STATISTICAL MATHEMATICS

A COMPANION TO 'A SECOND COURSE IN STATISTICS'

ROBERT LOVEDAY

M.Sc. (SHEFFIELD), F.I.S., F.I.M.A.

CAMBRIDGE
AT THE UNIVERSITY PRESS
1973

Published by the Syndics of the Cambridge University Press
Bentley House, 200 Euston Road, London NW1 2DB
American Branch: 32 East 57th Street, New York, N.Y.10022

ISBN: 0 521 08643 4

Printed in Great Britain
at the University Printing House, Cambridge
(Brooke Crutchley, University Printer)

CONTENTS

PREFACE

This small book is simply a mathematical companion to *A Second Course in Statistics* and for that reason it is called *Statistical Mathematics*. It results from the encouragement of many teachers and students. In their letters, users of my second course have asked for a supplementary volume to help them with the more searching aspects of the subject. 'Although I have been teaching mathematics for 18 years', writes one teacher, 'I am a novice in the teaching of statistics and have found considerable difficulty in writing answers to the more recent examination questions at Advanced and Scholarship level.'

This book assumes, then, that the reader is already familiar with the statistical ideas and methods of my earlier books and wishes to study further their mathematical background. It begins with a set of *Revision Exercises* to make sure the statistics are not forgotten. The *Glossary* of statistical terms, formulae and ideas at the end of the book is also an aid to the memory. The opening revision exercises are all taken from the examination papers set for the Diploma in Mathematics (Teaching) and I am grateful to the Mathematical Association for allowing me to reproduce them. Throughout the book questions from the examinations set by

The Institute of Statisticians, 55 Park Lane, London, W. 1,
The University of London B.Sc. (Economics) Examinations Council,
The University of Cambridge Local Examination Syndicate [Cambridge],
The Joint Matriculation Board [Northern],
The Associated Examining Board [A.E.B.],

have been used for examples and exercises and I thank these bodies sincerely for their permission to do this.

A great deal is taught by examples and exercises. A glance at *Miscellaneous Exercise* 27 will show that, right to the end, new methods of approach are being suggested. Also §6, Ex. 19, gives an idea of how a single exercise is used to teach definitions and ideas not otherwise included in the text.

My aim, as always, is to help my colleagues in the teaching profession. I dedicate the book to all the intelligent students it has been my privilege to teach at Ecclesfield Grammar School, 1931–42, Raynes Park High School 1942–58, Kingston Polytechnic 1958–69.

Finally my sincere thanks are due to the Syndics of the Cambridge University Press. I appreciate the great encouragement they have given me. Indeed the title of this book was the inspiration of one of the Syndics.

August 1972 R.L.

PRELIMINARY REVISION EXERCISES

The reader is advised to work through some of these exercises before beginning Chapter 1. The *Glossary* will be found useful.

1. The following table is a frequency distribution of the marks obtained by 800 candidates in an examination:

Examination mark	0–9	10–19	20–29	30–39	40–49
Number of candidates	14	35	93	113	167

Examination mark	50–59	60–69	70–79	80–89	90–99
Number of candidates	129	104	87	34	24

(i) By representing these data on probability paper, or otherwise, estimate the 20th, 50th and 90th percentiles. State the assumptions involved. Estimate also the percentile rank of a mark of 85. Explain how percentiles and percentile ranks are of use in assessing the results of examinations.

(ii) Calculate to the nearest integer, the mean and standard deviation of the above distribution. If the marks are to be adjusted so that the new mean is 55 and the new standard deviation 10 find a formula for the new mark, y, in terms of the old mark, x. Explain the purposes of such an adjustment.

2. (*a*) Consider the word ANTIBIOTIC.

(i) If all 10 letters are arranged in a row, how many different permutations are possible?

(ii) If 3 letters are chosen from the 10, how many different combinations are possible?

(iii) What is the probability that at least 2 of 3 letters selected at random from the 10 are Is?

(*b*) Of the total output of a factory 30 % is produced in workshop A and 70 % in workshop B. On the average, 12 components out of 1000 produced in A are defective and 8 out of 1000 produced in B are defective. If a component drawn at random from the whole output is defective, what is the probability that it is from workshop A?

3. For the n (x, y) pairs $(x_1, y_1), (x_2, y_2), \ldots, (x_n, y_n)$ with mean $(\bar{x}, \bar{y})$ prove that

$$\sum_{r=1}^{n} (x_r - \bar{x})(y_r - \bar{y}) = \sum_{r=1}^{n} x_r y_r - n\bar{x}\bar{y}.$$

x	180	168	168	161	164	152	148	144	149	140	134	128
y	11.0	11.2	11.4	12.0	12.8	13.4	13.6	14.0	15.0	15.0	15.4	16.0

In the above bivariate distribution x gives the age in months of 12 boys and y gives the time in seconds each boy takes to run 100 m.

Given that $\Sigma x = 1836$, $\Sigma y = 160.8$, $\Sigma x^2 = 283\,550$, $\Sigma y^2 = 2187.92$, $\Sigma xy = 24\,320.2$. Calculate

(i) the product–moment correlation coefficient and comment on the meaning of its sign,

(ii) the equation, in the form $y = a + bx$, of the least-squares line of regression of y on x.

Illustrate the original data and the regression line in graphical form and use the regression line to estimate the average number of metres by which a 14-year-old boy would beat an 11-year-old boy.

4. (*a*) In a certain subject the examination marks of the boys are Normally distributed about a mean 55 with standard deviation 11 and the marks of the girls are Normally distributed about a mean 58 with standard deviation 8. If one boy and one girl are chosen at random from the complete list of candidates determine

(i) the probability that the boy's mark is over 75,
(ii) the probability that the girl's mark is over 75,
(iii) the probability that the girl's mark is at least 20 more than the boy's,
(iv) the probability that the boy's mark is at least 20 more than the girl's.

(*b*) In another subject, the mean mark of a sample of 100 boys is 56 and that of 80 girls is 59. Assuming population standard deviations of 10 and 9 respectively determine whether the difference between these means is significant at the 5 % level.

5. (*a*) In a manufacturing process 4 % of the components produced are defective. If the production is controlled by drawing random samples of 40 show that a sample with 4 *or more* defectives can be expected less frequently than one occasion in ten.

(*b*) Over a long period in the past it has been established that 52 % of the candidates taking a certain qualifying test have passed. This year 60 candidates out of a random sample of 100 have been successful. Make calculations to decide if this is sufficient evidence, at the 5 % level of significance, to support the view that the percentage of passes has changed. Comment on the result of your calculations.

6. The following table is a frequency distribution of the marks obtained by 1200 candidates in Pure Mathematics:

Examination mark	0–9	10–19	20–29	30–39	40–49
Number of candidates	23	44	45	124	345

Examination mark	50–59	60–69	70–79	80–89	90–99
Number of candidates	267	189	119	37	7

(i) Estimate, graphically or otherwise, the median and quartiles of the distribution. State the assumptions involved. The marks of the same 1200 candidates in Applied Mathematics had a median 49 and quartiles 24 and 69. Explain how you would adjust, graphically or otherwise, the marks in Applied

Mathematics before adding them to the marks in Pure Mathematics and the purpose of such an adjustment.

(ii) Calculate the mean and the standard deviation of the above distribution of Pure Mathematics marks and use the Normal distribution tables to obtain the median and quartiles of a set of 1200 marks Normally distributed about the same mean with the same standard deviation.

7. (*a*) Of the 20 members of a tennis club, five are left-handed. A set of four players is chosen at random from the 20. Obtain the probability of at least two of the four players being left-handed.

(*b*) In a high jump trial in which A and B compete, the bar is raised inch by inch until one of the two competitors fails to clear it. If both competitors fail at the same height the trial is not recorded. In 10 of these trials it was recorded that A won eight times and B only twice. Make calculations to decide if this is sufficient evidence to reject, at the 5 % level, the hypothesis that A and B are equally good.

In another series of trials between C and D it was stated that the hypothesis of equality was rejected at the 5 % level because C had always failed first. What is the smallest number of trials that could have been recorded?

8. For the n (x, y) pairs $(x_1, y_1), (x_2, y_2), \ldots, (x_n, y_n)$ with mean $(\bar{x}, \bar{y})$ prove that

$$\sum_{r=1}^{n} (x_r - \bar{x})(y_r - \bar{y}) = \sum_{r=1}^{n} x_r y_r - n\bar{x}\bar{y}.$$

Suppose that (x_1, y_1) are the respective examination marks of a student at the end of his first and second year and that $(x_2, y_2), \ldots, (x_n, y_n)$, where $n = 30$, are the corresponding first and second year marks of 29 other students in the same class as the first student. Given that

$$\sum_{r=1}^{30} x_r = 1379, \quad \sum_{r=1}^{30} y_r = 1282, \quad \sum_{r=1}^{30} x_r y_r = 83853,$$

$$\sum_{r=1}^{30} x_r^2 = 89371, \quad \sum_{r=1}^{30} y_r^2 = 90488,$$

calculate, as accurately as your tables permit,

$$\sum_{r=1}^{30} (x_r - \bar{x})^2, \quad \sum_{r=1}^{30} (y_r - \bar{y})^2 \quad \text{and} \quad \sum_{r=1}^{30} (x_r - \bar{x})(y_r - \bar{y}).$$

Hence obtain:

(i) the product–moment correlation coefficient and comment on its meaning;
(ii) the equation, in the form $y = a + bx$, of the least-squares line of regression of y on x.

If a 31st student obtained 50 marks in the first examination but did not take the second, use the equation of (ii) above to estimate a second year mark for him and discuss the fairness of awarding such a mark.

9. (i) At one stage in the assembly of a machine, a cylindrical rod with circular cross-section of diameter d has to fit into a circular socket of diameter D. Measurement of a large number of these rods and sockets indicates that both d and D are Normally distributed about respective means 5.01 cm and 5.11 cm with respective standard deviations 0.03 cm and 0.04 cm. If components are selected at random for assembly, show that 2.28 % of the rods are likely to be too big for the socket for which they are chosen.

(ii) In the production of machines described in (i) above, assuming that 2.28 % of the rods are too big for the socket for which they are chosen, calculate the probability that, in 100 random fittings, less than three rods will be too big.

10. (i) Given that the probability of an event occurring in a single trial is $\frac{1}{3}$, calculate, to three significant figures, the respective probabilities $P(2)$, $P(4)$, $P(6)$ of 2, 4, 6 occurrences of the event in 18 independent trials.

(ii) Use the tabulated values of

$$\phi(x) = \frac{1}{\sqrt{(2\pi)}} e^{-\frac{1}{2}x^2}$$

to write down $\frac{1}{2}\phi(2)$, $\frac{1}{2}\phi(1)$, $\frac{1}{2}\phi(0)$ to three significant figures. Explain, fully, why the respective values of (i) are approximately equal to those of (ii).

11. (*a*) In an examination the distribution of the Arithmetic marks was approximately Normal about a mean mark of 52 with standard deviation 10 marks. Draw the frequency curve of the distribution taking a scale of 1 cm to represent 10 marks and making the total area under the curve 10 cm².

In the same examination the marks for English were distributed as follows:

English mark	20–29	30–39	40–49	50–59	60–69	70–79	80–89
Number of candidates	8	64	284	428	162	48	6

Using also a total area of 10 cm², and the same base scale as for Arithmetic marks, represent the distribution of English marks by a histogram superimposed on the frequency curve already drawn.

(*b*) On Arithmetic probability paper represent the above distribution of Arithmetic marks by a suitable straight line and then, in the same diagram using the same scales and axes, plot points to represent the cumulative percentage frequencies of the English marks. Explain how the points you have plotted indicate whether or not the English marks are Normally distributed.

12. Twenty boys are classified by their intelligence quotients as follows:

	A	*B*	*C*
Intelligence Quotient	over 110	90 to 110	less than 90
Number of boys	3	13	4

(*a*) How many arrangements of 6 of the boys are possible in the 6 seats on the back row of the class if 3 of the seats must be occupied by the 3 *A* boys and the other 3 seats may be occupied by any 3 of the other 17 boys?

(*b*) A committee is to be elected consisting of a Chairman and a Secretary who must be *A* boys and 4 other members who must be *B* or *C* boys. How many selections, such as this, are possible?

(*c*) If 3 boys are chosen at random from the 20 what is the probability that
(i) all 3 are *A* boys?
(ii) there is 1 boy from each of the 3 groups *A*, *B*, *C*?
(iii) one, and only one, is an *A* boy?

13. The *Infant Mortality* rate is the number of deaths of infants under 1 year of age per thousand live births. In the following table, extracted from the *Annual Abstract of Statistics*, x is the year with 1940 as origin and y the Infant Mortality rate of the U.K. for that year. In the table values of $Y = \log_e y$ are also included.

Year	1940	1945	1950	1955	1960	1965
x	0	5	10	15	20	25
y	61.0	48.8	31.2	25.8	22.4	20.0
$Y = \log_e y$	4.111	3.888	3.441	3.250	3.109	2.996

Given that $\Sigma x = 75$, $\Sigma Y = 20.795$, $\Sigma x^2 = 1375$, $\Sigma xY = 239.68$ and assuming that the relationship between x and Y is approximately linear, use the method of least squares to obtain the best values of a and b in the equation $Y = a+bx$ connecting x and Y.

Deduce the constants A and k in the equation $y = Ae^{-kx}$ estimating y from a given x and calculate this value of y for 1985.

14. (*a*) A swimming instructor claims that he can teach 60 % of non-swimmers to swim the breadth of the baths in 6 lessons. Assuming this claim to be true and also that the probability of any non-swimmer being successful is independent of the probabilities of the other non-swimmers in the class being successful, calculate for a class of 10 pupils

(i) the probability of more than 8 non-swimmers,
(ii) the probability of less than 2 non-swimmers
learning to swim the breadth in 6 lessons.

(*b*) State briefly the circumstances in which a Normal distribution is a close approximation to a Binomial distribution.

Out of 100 non-swimmers taught by the instructor of (*a*) above only 50 learn to swim the breadth in 6 lessons. Make calculations to decide if this provides sufficient evidence to reject, at the 5 % level of significance, the instructor's claim.

15. (*a*) The mean, μ_x, and the variance, σ_x^2, of the n values x_r $(r = 1, 2, \ldots, n)$ are defined by

$$\mu_x = \frac{1}{n}\sum_{r=1}^{n} x_r \quad \text{and} \quad \sigma_x^2 = \frac{1}{n}\sum_{r=1}^{n} (x_r - \mu_x)^2.$$

Show that

$$\sigma_x^2 = \frac{1}{n}\sum_{r=1}^{n} x_r^2 - \mu_x^2.$$

Given a set of 4 numbers x_i $(i = 1, 2, 3, 4)$ and a second set of 3 numbers y_j $(j = 1, 2, 3)$ write down the set of 12 numbers represented by $z_{ij} = x_i - y_j$. Hence show that $\mu_z = \mu_x - \mu_y$ and $\sigma_z^2 = \sigma_x^2 + \sigma_y^2$.

(*b*) The heights of boys in a certain age group are Normally distributed about a mean 160 cm with standard deviation 4 cm; the heights of girls in the same age group are Normally distributed about a mean 156 cm with standard deviation 3 cm. If a boy and a girl are chosen at random, determine the probability that the girl is taller than the boy.

16. (*a*) When planning a ten-day holiday tour a motorist estimated the distance, x km, he would go each day by measuring the daily journey as a straight line on his map and taking x to the nearest 50. During the tour he recorded the actual daily distance y km. The values x and y are tabulated below together with the ratios $z = y/x$. Calculate the mean value of z and the standard deviation.

Day	Estimated distance x km (nearest 50 km)	Actual distance y km (nearest integer)	Ratio $z = y/x$
1	250	305	1.22
2	150	243	1.62
3	100	162	1.62
4	250	290	1.16
5	100	149	1.49
6	250	295	1.18
7	300	387	1.29
8	400	448	1.12
9	250	325	1.30
10	250	375	1.50

For a *Normal* distribution of ratios $z = y/x$ with the same mean and standard deviation as the above sample find the probability of the actual distance being between 130 and 140 km when its estimate is 100 km.

(*b*) In order to test the hypothesis that ratios such as z are Normally distributed a teacher asked a hundred pupils to measure the distances, in metres, of their homes from school as straight lines on a map and then to measure the actual distances along the road. Describe the steps to be taken with the hundred values of z thus obtained to verify in some way that z is probably a Normal variable. Discuss whether or not a Normal distribution of z in the school experiment would justify the assumption of Normality in the case of the motorist.

17. Consider the 17 letters

ALL SHAPES AND SIZES

(*a*) If three letters are chosen from the 17, how many *different* selections are possible?

(*b*) If three letters are drawn at random from the 17, calculate the probability that (i) all three letters are the same, (ii) two of the three letters are the same, (iii) all three letters are different.

18. The height, x mm, and the weight, y kg, of each boy in a school were recorded and a scatter diagram was then plotted. State, with reasons, which of the two possible regression lines is likely to prove the more useful.

The equation of the line of regression of y on x is found to be

$$y = 0.08x - 80.$$

If the heights are distributed about a mean of 1600 mm with standard deviation 120 mm and the standard deviation of the weights is 12 kg find

(i) the mean of the weights,
(ii) the equation of the line of regression of x on y,
(iii) the coefficient of correlation.

19. A new method of treating rheumatoid-arthritis in children has been developed and its probability of success is claimed to be 70 %. ('Success' in this case means that, after treatment, a child is able to lead a full normal life.) Show that if 10 children are treated by this method the chance of more than seven successes is about 38 %.

By using the Normal distribution table, or otherwise, show that for a group of 20 children the chance of the number of successes being outside the range 10 to 18 is about 5 %.

20. The table below expresses in statistical terms a summary of a statement made in casual conversation by a man who travels regularly from the Victoria Air Terminal, London, to an office near the Empire State Building, New York.

	Mean time (hours)	Standard deviation (hours)
Bus Journey from Victoria to Heathrow	0.5	0.1
Wait at Heathrow airport before take-off	1.5	0.3
Flight from Heathrow to the vicinity of Kennedy airport	7.0	0.5
Time waiting in the air for permission to land together with landing time	0.5	0.2
Wait at Kennedy airport	0.5	0.2
Bus journey from Kennedy to Empire State Building	0.5	0.2

Assuming that all the times are Normally and independently distributed show that the chance of travelling from Victoria to the Empire State Building in under 10 hours is less than a quarter.

21. Distribution of the population of the U.K. in 1966 shown as percentages of the total, 54 millions. (Source: Annual Abstract of Statistics 1968)

Age	Percentage of total population
under 1	1.8
1 and under 2	1.8
2–4	5.2
5–9	7.8
10–14	7.1
15–19	7.8
20–29	12.6
30–39	12.1
40–59	25.9
60–99	17.9
Total	100.0

Represent the above data by a histogram. Ignoring the possibility of death, use the histogram or the original data to estimate, as a percentage of 54 millions, how many children will reach the age of 11 in 1971. Estimate also the alterations in this percentage during the years 1972, 1973, ..., 1977. State how these alterations contrast with those for young people reaching the age of 21 in the years 1971, 1972, ..., 1978.

22. A box contains 12 car components all of which appear to be exactly the same. Actually, 3 of the 12 will require a slight adjustment before use. If 4 components are taken at random from the box, calculate the probability that the number which will require adjustment is (i) 0, (ii) 1, (iii) 2, (iv) 3.

23. A certain disease which was previously regarded as incurable is now being treated by a new method which, it is claimed, will effect a cure in $16\frac{2}{3}$ % of all cases treated. If 12 sufferers from the disease are given this new treatment, what is the probability that the number of cures is (i) 2, (ii) less than 2, (iii) more than 2?

State the mean and the standard deviation of the probability distribution of the number of cures when 60 sufferers are given the new treatment and, by using the Normal distribution table, estimate the probability of the number of cures being 5 or less.

24. A general knowledge test consisting of 100 questions was given to all the pupils of a school. The following table shows the number of correct answers by the best 11-year-old, the best 12-year-old, the best 13-year-old, etc.

Mid-interval value of the age-group x	Number of correct answers by the best pupil of the group y
$11\frac{1}{2}$	18
$12\frac{1}{2}$	25
$13\frac{1}{2}$	29
$14\frac{1}{2}$	27
$15\frac{1}{2}$	31
$16\frac{1}{2}$	40
$17\frac{1}{2}$	35
$18\frac{1}{2}$	43

Calculate, in the form $y = a+bx$, the equation of the line of regression of y on x and also the correlation coefficient, r_{xy}, all coefficients being correct to three significant figures.

After taking age into account, a cup is to be awarded to the age-group which provided the individual with the most outstanding performance. Draw a graph of the original data together with the regression line and use it to decide by inspection which age-group should receive the cup. State briefly your reasons.

25.

Time of car journey in minutes (to nearest minute)	Frequency
18–20	10
21–23	24
24–26	38
27–29	23
30–32	4
33–35	1

The above table is the frequency distribution of the times of 100 car journeys made by a teacher from his home to school, a distance of $7\frac{1}{2}$ miles in a built-up area. Show that the mean and the standard deviation, to the nearest integer, are 25 minutes and 3 minutes respectively.

Some time later, after the introduction of a one-way traffic system over part of the journey, the mean of the times of 50 journeys was found to be 23 minutes, the standard deviation being unaltered. Determine whether or not a reduction of these sample means from 25 to 23 minutes with standard deviation 3 minutes is significant at the $2\frac{1}{2}\%$ level.

1

CONTINUOUS DISTRIBUTIONS

1. Properties of continuous distributions. The equation of the Normal density function in its most general form is

$$y = \frac{1}{\sigma\sqrt{(2\pi)}}\, e^{-\frac{1}{2}(x-\mu)^2/\sigma^2}.$$

Here, x varies continuously from $-\infty$ to $+\infty$, μ is the mean, σ the standard deviation and the distribution is called *Normal* (μ, σ^2). It is one of many *continuous probability distributions* of the form $y = f(x)$ which are important because they provide mathematical models for the frequency distributions obtained from observed data, many examples of which have been met in earlier studies. In this general form, $f(x)$ is a continuous non-negative function of x called the *probability density function* (sometimes the *relative frequency function*) and the graph of $y = f(x)$ is the *probability curve* which models the frequency polygon drawn from observed data. The range of the *random variable* or *variate*, x, is not necessarily infinite. The statement

$$\begin{aligned} y &= f(x), \quad \text{if} \quad a \leqslant x \leqslant b, \\ &= 0, \qquad \text{otherwise,} \end{aligned}$$

implies that the function under consideration has non-negative values when x lies in the range (a, b) but is zero when x lies outside that range. The area under the graph of $y = f(x)$ represents the total probability and is, therefore, unity. Thus

$$\int_{-\infty}^{\infty} f(x)\,dx = 1.$$

The *relative frequency* with which values of the variate are observed in the range $(x-\frac{1}{2}dx)$ to $(x+\frac{1}{2}dx)$ is $f(x)dx$.* Alternatively we may state that the *probability* of the variate falling in the range $(x-\frac{1}{2}dx)$ to $(x+\frac{1}{2}dx)$ is $f(x)dx$ and we write

$$dp = f(x)\,dx.$$

Thus the Normal (μ, σ^2) probability function may be written

$$dp = \frac{1}{\sigma\sqrt{(2\pi)}}\, e^{-\frac{1}{2}(x-\mu)^2/\sigma^2}\,dx.$$

* The range is stated this way rather than as x to $x+dx$ in order to anticipate the correction for continuity of §37.

2. Cumulative distribution function. Suppose an experiment is performed and a certain numerical result is obtained. It is more logical to denote this number in general by the capital letter X and to reserve the small letter x for the continuous variable of the probability density function $f(x)$. Thus

$$P(\alpha \leqslant X \leqslant \beta) = \int_{x=\alpha}^{x=\beta} \mathrm{d}p = \int_{\alpha}^{\beta} f(x)\,\mathrm{d}x$$

is the probability that the random variable or variate, X, falls in the interval (α, β) and it is represented graphically by the area under the probability curve, $y = f(x)$, between the ordinates $x = \alpha$ and $x = \beta$. Moreover, if X is a continuous random variable with probability density function $f(x)$ then

$$\begin{aligned} F(x) &= P(X \leqslant x) \\ &= \int_{-\infty}^{x} f(x)\,\mathrm{d}x \end{aligned}$$

is defined as the *cumulative distribution function* of X, or more simply as the *distribution function* of X.

In the *Cambridge Elementary Statistical Tables* by D. V. Lindley and J. C. P. Miller the values of the Normal (0, 1) distribution

$$\phi(x) = \frac{1}{\sqrt{(2\pi)}}\,\mathrm{e}^{-\frac{1}{2}x^2}$$

and also the values of the cumulative Normal (0, 1) distribution

$$\Phi(x) = \int_{-\infty}^{x} \phi(t)\,\mathrm{d}t$$

are tabulated. Hence, if the random variable X is distributed Normally about a zero mean with unit standard deviation the probability that it falls within the interval (α, β) may be deduced from these tables as

$$P(\alpha \leqslant X \leqslant \beta) = \int_{\alpha}^{\beta} \phi(x)\,\mathrm{d}x = \Phi(\beta) - \Phi(\alpha).$$

This probability may also be obtained graphically by using arithmetic probability graph paper.

The probability statements

$$P(\alpha < X < \beta), \quad P(\alpha \leqslant X < \beta), \quad P(\alpha < X \leqslant \beta) \quad \text{and} \quad P(\alpha \leqslant X \leqslant \beta)$$

are all equivalent because the probability that a continuous variable is equal to a specific numerical value is zero; that is to say $P(X = \alpha) = 0$ and $P(X = \beta) = 0$ since $P(X = \alpha)$ and $P(X = \beta)$ are respectively

$$\int_{\alpha}^{\alpha} f(x)\,\mathrm{d}x \quad \text{and} \quad \int_{\beta}^{\beta} f(x)\,\mathrm{d}x.$$

3. Moments of a continuous distribution. If

$$\begin{aligned} y &= f(x), \quad a \leqslant x \leqslant b, \\ &= 0, \qquad \text{otherwise}, \end{aligned}$$

is a continuous probability function then, by definition

$$\int_a^b y \mathrm{d}x = 1,$$

and the first, second, third and fourth moments about *zero* are respectively

$$\nu_1 = \int_a^b xy \mathrm{d}x, \quad \nu_2 = \int_a^b x^2 y \mathrm{d}x, \quad \nu_3 = \int_a^b x^3 y \mathrm{d}x \quad \text{and} \quad \nu_4 = \int_a^b x^4 y \mathrm{d}x.$$

The first moment about zero, ν_1, is the mean μ (or $\bar{x}$) of the distribution and the first, second, third and fourth moments about the *mean* μ are respectively

$$\mu_1 = \int_a^b (x-\mu)\, y \mathrm{d}x = 0,$$

$$\mu_2 = \int_a^b (x-\mu)^2\, y \mathrm{d}x = \nu_2 - \nu_1^2,$$

$$\mu_3 = \int_a^b (x-\mu)^3\, y \mathrm{d}x = \nu_3 - 3\nu_2\nu_1 + 2\nu_1^3$$

and

$$\mu_4 = \int_a^b (x-\mu)^4\, y \mathrm{d}x = \nu_4 - 4\nu_3\nu_1 + 6\nu_2\nu_1^2 - 3\nu_1^4.$$

It is assumed that the reader will have no difficulty in establishing these results.

Thus the mean μ and the variance σ^2 of the distribution are respectively

$$\mu = \int_a^b xy \mathrm{d}x \quad \text{and} \quad \sigma^2 = \int_a^b x^2 y \mathrm{d}x - \mu^2.$$

4. Percentiles of a continuous distribution. If p_{50} is the value of x such that

$$P(a \leqslant X \leqslant p_{50}) = \int_a^{p_{50}} y \mathrm{d}x = 0.50,$$

then p_{50} is the *50th percentile* or *median* of the distribution. Similarly p_{25} such that

$$P(a \leqslant X \leqslant p_{25}) = \int_a^{p_{25}} y \mathrm{d}x = 0.25$$

is the 25th percentile or *lower quartile* of the distribution and p_{75} such that

$$P(a \leqslant X \leqslant p_{75}) = \int_a^{p_{75}} y \mathrm{d}x = 0.75$$

is the 75th percentile or *upper quartile* of the distribution. In general the nth percentile p_n is given by

$$P(a \leqslant X \leqslant p_n) = \int_a^{p_n} y\,dx = n/100.$$

5. Mode of a continuous distribution. The *mode* (modes) of the probability density function $y = f(x)$ is (are) the value (values) of x for which y is a maximum. The exercises which follow contain examples of the methods of determining the mode.

6. Exercises.

The reader will find many important ideas and well-known facts established in the following exercises.

1. (i) If $$\phi(x) = \frac{1}{\sqrt{(2\pi)}}\, e^{-\frac{1}{2}x^2},$$
show that $x^n\phi(x) \to 0$ when $x \to \infty$.

(ii) For the Normal (μ, σ^2) distribution

$$y = \frac{1}{\sigma\sqrt{(2\pi)}}\, e^{-\frac{1}{2}(x-\mu)^2/\sigma^2},$$

by substituting $t = (x-\mu)/\sigma$, show that

$$\int_{-\infty}^{\infty} (x-\mu)^n\, y\,dx = \sigma^n \int_{-\infty}^{\infty} t^n \phi(t)\,dt.$$

Hence, by assuming that $$\int_{-\infty}^{\infty} \phi(x)\,dx = 1,$$

show that the first, second, third and fourth moments about the mean are respectively $$\mu_1 = 0,\quad \mu_2 = \sigma^2,\quad \mu_3 = 0,\quad \mu_4 = 3\sigma^4.$$

This establishes the moments test *for Normality that*

$$\beta_1 = \mu_3^2/\mu_2^3 = 0 \quad \textit{and} \quad \beta_2 = \mu_4/\mu_2^2 = 3.$$

(N.B. These two conditions are necessary but *not* sufficient.)

(iii) By means of a diagram, or otherwise, show that

$$\int_{-\infty}^{\infty} |x|\,\phi(x)\,dx = 2\int_0^{\infty} x\phi(x)\,dx.$$

Hence show that the *mean deviation* of the Normal (0, 1) distribution

$$\int_{-\infty}^{\infty} |x|\,\phi(x)\,dx = \sqrt{(2/\pi)}.$$

This indicates that the mean deviation of a Normal distribution is approximately $\frac{4}{5}$ of the standard deviation.

(iv) Use statistical tables, such as those of Lindley and Miller, to obtain the upper quartile, p_{75}, and the lower quartile, p_{25}, of the Normal (0, 1) distribution. Hence show that the semi-interquartile range or quartile deviation $\frac{1}{2}(p_{75}-p_{25}) = 0.675$, correct to three decimal places. Thus, *for Normal distributions the quartile deviation is approximately $\frac{2}{3}$ of the standard deviation.*

2. The continuous random variable X is said to be *uniformly* (or *rectangularly*) distributed in the interval (a, b) if its probability density function is given by

$$f(x) = \frac{1}{b-a}, \quad a \leqslant x \leqslant b,$$
$$= 0, \qquad \text{otherwise.}$$

Sketch the probability graph and obtain:

(i) the cumulative distribution function $F(x) = P(X \leqslant x)$,
(ii) the mean and variance.

3. The continuous random variable X is said to have an *Exponential distribution* with parameter $\lambda > 0$ if its probability density function is given by

$$f(x) = \lambda e^{-\lambda x}, \quad x \geqslant 0,$$
$$= 0, \qquad x < 0.$$

Sketch the probability curve and obtain

(i) the cumulative distribution function $F(x) = P(X \leqslant x)$,
(ii) the mean, median, mode and variance.

4. A random variable, X, has for its frequency (probability density) function $f(x)$ where

$$f(x) = 4(x-1)(2-x)(3-x), \quad \text{if } 1 < x < 2,$$
$$= 0, \qquad \text{otherwise.}$$

Find the mean and variance of X.

What is the probability that a value of X taken at random will exceed 1.8? [A.E.B.]

5. A random variable, X, has for its probability density function $f(x)$ where

$$f(x) = A(6-x)(x-2), \quad \text{if } 2 \leqslant x \leqslant 6,$$
$$f(x) = 0, \qquad \text{if } x < 2 \text{ or } x > 6,$$

and A is constant.

Find the constant A and the mean and variance of X. [A.E.B.]

6. A variate X has positive values only and its probability density is $\frac{1}{2}x^2 e^{-x}$.
Sketch the probability curve of X.
Find the mean and variance of X. [A.E.B.]

7. If n is a positive integer, show that

(i) $$\frac{x^n}{e^x} \to 0 \quad \text{when} \quad x \to \infty,$$

(ii) $$\int_0^\infty x^n e^{-x}\,dx = n!$$

A variate X is distributed between 0 and ∞ with a probability distribution

$$p(x)\,\mathrm{d}x = \frac{x^n \mathrm{e}^{-x}}{n!}\,\mathrm{d}x.$$

Calculate the mean value of X and its variance. [Northern]

8. The random variable X has probability density given by the curve

$$y = \frac{x^n \mathrm{e}^{-x}}{n!},$$

where n is an integer and x goes from zero to infinity. Show that the *mode* (i.e. the value of x when y is a maximum) is n.

When $n = 3$, find the probability that a random value of x exceeds the mode. [A.E.B.]

9. A continuous variable X has frequency function $f(x)$. Define the distribution function (cumulative frequency function) $F(x)$ and show how it is used in expressing the proportion of observations of X which may be expected to lie in any range (a, b). Sketch the typical form of $F(x)$. Why cannot the graph of a distribution function have a negative gradient?

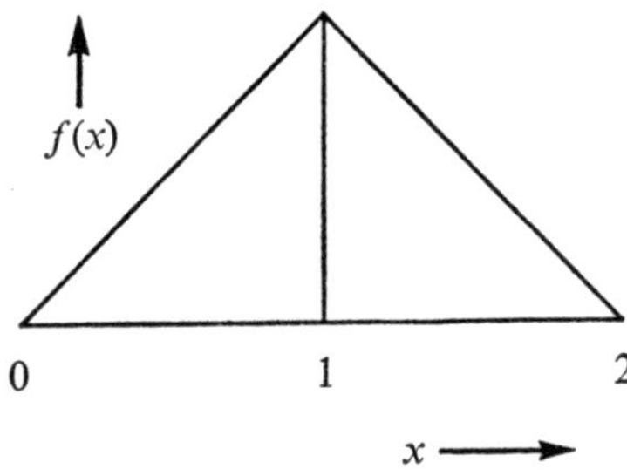

Obtain $F(x)$ for $0 \leqslant X \leqslant 1$, where $f(x)$ is as shown in the figure, and sketch $F(x)$ for $0 \leqslant x \leqslant 3$. [Cambridge]

10. The cumulative frequency function $F(x)$ of a continuous positive variable X takes values from 0 to 1. Explain how you could derive, from the curve $y = F(x)$, the median and the mode (or modes) of the distribution; and show that the mean is the area bounded by the curve and the lines $x = 0$, $y = 0$ and $y = 1$.

What property of the curve of $F(x)$ corresponds to symmetry of $f(x)$, the frequency distribution? Show that for such a distribution:

(*a*) the mean and the median are the same, and equal to the mode if there is only one; and

(*b*) the median is midway between the quartiles.

Show by a sketch that statement (*b*) can be true for a skew distribution. [Cambridge]

11. The life times, X hours, of radio valves have the continuous probability density function

$$f(x) = \begin{cases} \frac{1}{1000}\mathrm{e}^{-x/1000}, & x \geqslant 0, \\ 0, & x < 0. \end{cases}$$

An amplifier contains five valves, the life time of each having the above distribution. The makers guarantee that not more than two valves will have to be replaced during the first 1000 hours of use. Find the probability that the guarantee is violated, assuming that the valves wear out independently. [Northern]

12. A garage is supplied with petrol once a week. The weekly demand X, in millions of litres, has the continuous probability density function

$$f(x) = \begin{cases} 5(1-x)^4, & 0 \leqslant x \leqslant 1, \\ 0, & \text{otherwise.} \end{cases}$$

What must be the total capacity of the petrol tanks if the probability that they will be exhausted in any given week is to be only 0.01? [Northern]

13. Write down the conditions which must be satisfied by any probability density function (pdf).

The function

$$\begin{aligned} f(x) &= k\{a-(x-b)^2\}, \quad -1 \leqslant x \leqslant 1, k > 0, \\ &= 0, \qquad\qquad\qquad \text{otherwise,} \end{aligned}$$

is a pdf with zero mean. Find b and the range of possible values of a, and express k in terms of a. Determine the value of a for which the variance of the distribution has its smallest possible value. [Northern]

14. Show that $$\int_0^\infty t^n \mathrm{e}^{-t}\,\mathrm{d}t = n\int_0^\infty t^{n-1}\mathrm{e}^{-t}\,\mathrm{d}t \quad \text{if} \quad n > 0,$$

and that $$\int_0^\infty \mathrm{e}^{-t}\,\mathrm{d}t = 1.$$

Hence evaluate $$\int_0^\infty t^n \mathrm{e}^{-t}\,\mathrm{d}t$$

when n is a positive integer. [A.E.B.]

15. A random variable has the frequency function

$$f(y) = cy\mathrm{e}^{-2y}, \quad 0 \leqslant y \leqslant \infty.$$

Find c and calculate the mean of the distribution.

Given two independent observations from this distribution, what is the probability that one of them is greater than the mean and one of them is less than the mean? [London B.Sc. Econ.]

16. Three independent observations are drawn from the distribution

$$f(y) = cye^{-y}, \quad 0 \leqslant y \leqslant \infty.$$

Find c and the mean of the distribution.

What is the probability that at least two observations are greater than the mean?

What is the probability that exactly two observations fall in the interval $1 \leqslant y \leqslant 3$? [London B.Sc. Econ.]

17. A random variable Y has the probability density function $f(y) = y^2+by+1$, $0 \leqslant y \leqslant 1$.

Find the value of b.

What is the probability that in a random sample of 4 observations:

(*a*) 3 or more observations are greater than the mean,
(*b*) exactly 2 observations are greater than the median.

[London B.Sc. Econ.]

18. If the third moment, μ_3, is *zero* the distribution is *symmetrical*. If μ_3 is *negative* the distribution has a longer tail to the left of the mode than to the right and we say that the distribution is *skewed negatively*. If a distribution is more sharply peaked than Normal it is said to have an *excess of kurtosis* and is called *leptokurtic*. If a distribution is flat-topped and short-tailed compared with the Normal distribution it is *lacking in kurtosis* and called *platykurtic*. The fourth moment, μ_4, is used to measure kurtosis.

For Normal distributions $\mu_4 = 3\mu_2^2$ (see Ex. 1);
for leptokurtic distributions $\mu_4 > 3\mu_2^2$;
for platykurtic distributions $\mu_4 < 3\mu_2^2$.
Calculate μ_2, μ_3 and μ_4 for the distribution

$$\begin{aligned} f(x) &= A(3-x), \quad 0 \leqslant x \leqslant 3, \\ &= 0, \qquad\qquad \text{otherwise,} \end{aligned}$$

where A is a constant to be determined and hence comment on the skewness and kurtosis.

2

EXPECTATION

In *Statistics: A Second Edition of a Second Course*, Chapter 9, several important theorems were accepted and used for examples and exercises after they had been verified numerically. They will now be established by a more formal treatment.

7. Expectation of a continuous random variable. The word *mean* should only be used when averaging a set of observed values. The mean value of a complete theoretical distribution is called the *expected value* or the *mathematical expectation.* Thus, if X is a continuous random variable with probability density function $f(x)$ we write

$$\begin{aligned}\mu &= \int_{-\infty}^{\infty} xf(x)\,\mathrm{d}x \\ &= \text{the expectation of } X \\ &= E(X).\end{aligned}$$

8. Expectation of a discrete random variable. The Binomial distribution is an example of a *discrete* random variable X which takes the values $0, 1, 2, \ldots, r, \ldots, n$ with respective probabilities

$$P(X=0), P(X=1), P(X=2), \ldots, P(X=r), \ldots, P(X=n).$$

In general the values taken by a discrete random variable are not necessarily integers and, therefore, it is more logical to assume that X takes the discrete values

$$x_0, x_1, x_2, \ldots, x_r. \ldots. x_n,$$

with probabilities

$$P(X=x_0), P(X=x_1), P(X=x_2), \ldots, P(X=x_r), \ldots, P(X=x_n).$$

When describing a discrete random variable, however, it is often convenient to call it R and to write its probability distribution

$$p_0, p_1, p_2, \ldots, p_r, \ldots, p_n$$

as an abbreviation for

$$P(R=0), P(R=1), P(R=2), \ldots, P(R=r), \ldots, P(R=n).$$

This distinguishes it clearly from the continuous variable X with probability density function $f(x)$. Thus we write

$$\begin{aligned} \mu &= \text{the expectation of } R \\ &= E(R) \\ &= \sum_{\text{all } r} r p_r. \end{aligned}$$

9. Expectation of a function of a random variable. In E-notation the variance of the random variable X is defined by

$$\begin{aligned} \sigma^2 &= \text{var}(X) \\ &= E\{X-E(X)\}^2 \\ &= \int_{-\infty}^{\infty} (x-\mu)^2 f(x)\,\mathrm{d}x \quad \text{for continuous random variables,} \\ \text{or} \quad & \sum_{\text{all } r} (r-\mu)^2 p_r \quad \text{for discrete random variables.} \end{aligned}$$

This definition illustrates the fundamentally important idea that expectation is not limited to the random variable itself but that it applies also to functions of a random variable and, in general, we state

$$\begin{aligned} E\{g(X)\} &= \int_{-\infty}^{\infty} g(x) f(x)\,\mathrm{d}x \quad \text{for continuous variables} \\ \text{or} \quad & \sum_{\text{all } r} g(r) p_r \quad \text{for discrete variables.} \end{aligned}$$

10. The meaning of expectation. If a single die is cast the score, R, may be 1, 2, 3, 4, 5 or 6 and, assuming each score is equally probable, $E(R) = 3\frac{1}{2}$. This simple example stresses the fundamental fact that $E(R)$ is *not* the outcome we would expect when the experiment is performed once only. Indeed, in the above situation, $E(R)$ is not even a *possible* outcome. If, however, the die is cast a large number of times the mean of the various scores will become close to $3\frac{1}{2}$ although it may never become exactly $3\frac{1}{2}$.

11. The average of a sample and the expectation of a population. The last paragraph provides an example of the relationship between the processes of averaging in a sample and taking expectation in a population. In general let us consider the average of a discrete random variable R in a sample with typical frequency f_r when $R = r$.

The average or mean value of r

$$m = \frac{\Sigma r f_r}{\Sigma f_r} = \Sigma \left\{ r \left(\frac{f_r}{\Sigma f_r} \right) \right\},$$

the summations being taken over the full range of values of r. As the sample size Σf_r increases, the relative frequency of r, $(f_r/\Sigma f_r)$, approaches

p_r, the population probability for $R = r$. Thus the sample average approaches Σrp_r, the expectation of R. The relationship between average and expectation, therefore, corresponds to that between sample and population.

12. Properties of expected values. Some important properties of the expected values of random variables are as follows:

(i) If $X = C$ where C is constant, then

$$E(X) = C.$$

(ii) If C is constant, then

$$E(CX) = CE(X).$$

(iii) If X and Y are any two random variables

$$E(X+Y) = E(X)+E(Y).$$

(iv) If X and Y are any two *independent* random variables

$$E(XY) = E(X)\,E(Y).$$

Properties (i) and (ii) are so obvious that their proof is left as an exercise for the reader. Properties (iii) and (iv) are proved in §§13–16.

13. The expectation of the sum of two discrete random variables is equal to the sum of their expectations. Suppose that the discrete random variable X takes the values $x_1, x_2, \ldots, x_m$ with respective probabilities $p_1, p_2, \ldots, p_m$ and that the discrete random variable Y takes the values $y_1, y_2, \ldots, y_n$ with respective probabilities $q_1, q_2, \ldots, q_n$. The sum $(X+Y)$ can then take the mn values (x_i+y_j) where $i = 1, 2, \ldots, m$ and $j = 1, 2, \ldots, n$ because any of the m values of i may be associated with any of the n values of j. The probability that X takes the value x_i and, at the same time, Y takes the value y_j is called the *joint* probability of x_i and y_j. Let it be represented by p_{ij}. Then

$$\sum_{j=1}^{n} p_{ij} = p_i$$

because it is the sum of the probabilities that X assumes the value x_i while Y assumes the values $y_1, y_2, \ldots, y_n$. Similarly

$$\sum_{i=1}^{m} p_{ij} = q_j.$$

Thus

$$\begin{aligned} E(X+Y) &= \sum_{i=1}^{m} \sum_{j=1}^{n} p_{ij}(x_i+y_j) \\ &= \sum_{i=1}^{m} \left\{\sum_{j=1}^{n} p_{ij}\right\} x_i + \sum_{j=1}^{n} \left\{\sum_{i=1}^{m} p_{ij}\right\} y_j \\ &= \sum_{i=1}^{m} p_i x_i + \sum_{j=1}^{n} q_j y_j \\ &= E(X)+E(Y). \end{aligned}$$

By a change of sign throughout, the same argument establishes that

$$E(X-Y) = E(X)-E(Y).$$

Also, by applying mathematical induction, we can prove that

$$E(X_1+X_2+\ldots+X_n) = E(X_1)+E(X_2)+\ldots+E(X_n)$$

for n random variables, and in general, if $a_1, a_2, \ldots, a_n$ are constants, it is easy to deduce that

$$E(a_1 X_1+a_2 X_2+\ldots+a_n X_n) = a_1 E(X_1)+a_2 E(X_2)+\ldots+a_n E(X_n).$$

14. The expectation of the sum of two continuous random variables is equal to the sum of their expectations. Suppose the continuous random variables X and Y have respective probability density functions $f(x)$ and $g(y)$ such that

$$\int_{x_1}^{x_2} f(x)\,dx = 1 \quad \text{and} \quad \int_{y_1}^{y_2} g(y)\,dy = 1.$$

The sum $(X+Y)$ is then a two-dimensional random variable with a *joint* probability density function of x and y which may be represented by $h(x, y)$ where

$$\int_{x_1}^{x_2}\int_{y_1}^{y_2} h(x, y)\,dx\,dy = 1.$$

Thus

$$\begin{aligned} E(X+Y) &= \int_{x_1}^{x_2}\int_{y_1}^{y_2} (x+y)\, h(x, y)\,dx\,dy \\ &= \int_{x_1}^{x_2} x \left\{\int_{y_1}^{y_2} h(x, y)\,dy\right\} dx + \int_{y_1}^{y_2} y \left\{\int_{x_1}^{x_2} h(x, y)\,dx\right\} dy \\ &= \int_{x_1}^{x_2} x f(x)\,dx + \int_{y_1}^{y_2} y g(y)\,dy \\ &= E(X)+E(Y). \end{aligned}$$

15. The expectation of the product of two independent discrete random variables is the product of their expectations. Suppose that X and Y are two independent random variables such that X assumes the m values x_i with probabilities p_i $(i = 1, 2, \ldots, m)$ while Y assumes the n values y_j with probabilities q_j $(j = 1, 2, \ldots, n)$. Because p_i and q_j are independent, the probability that the product will assume the particular value $x_i y_j$ is $p_i q_j$. Hence the expectation of the product

$$E(XY) = \sum_{i=1}^{m}\sum_{j=1}^{n} x_i y_j p_i q_j.$$

Summing first with respect to j we obtain

$$E(XY) = \sum_{i=1}^{m} x_i p_i E(Y);$$

and then with respect to i we obtain

$$E(XY) = E(X)\,E(Y).$$

16. The expectation of the product of two independent continuous random variables is the product of their expectations. Suppose the continuous random variables X and Y have respective probability density functions $f(x)$ and $g(y)$ such that

$$\int_{x_1}^{x_2} f(x)\,\mathrm{d}x = 1 \quad \text{and} \quad \int_{y_1}^{y_2} g(y)\,\mathrm{d}y = 1.$$

Because X and Y are independent, the compound probability that X lies in the interval $\mathrm{d}x$ and Y lies in the interval $\mathrm{d}y$ is $f(x)\,\mathrm{d}x\,g(y)\,\mathrm{d}y$. Hence the expectation of the product

$$\begin{aligned} E(XY) &= \int_{x_1}^{x_2}\int_{y_1}^{y_2} f(x)g(y)\,\mathrm{d}x\,\mathrm{d}y \\ &= \int_{x_1}^{x_2} f(x)\,\mathrm{d}x\,E(Y) \\ &= E(X)\,E(Y). \end{aligned}$$

17. Moments by *E*-notation. In §3 certain methods of calculating moments were established for continuous distributions. By applying the ideas of expectation elegant proofs of these methods can be obtained. Thus

$$\begin{aligned} \sigma^2 &= E[\{X-E(X)\}^2] \\ &= E[X^2-2XE(X)+\{E(X)\}^2] \\ &= E(X^2)-2E(X)\,[E(X)]+\{E(X)\}^2 \\ &= E(X^2)-\{E(X)\}^2. \end{aligned}$$

Also the third moment about the mean

$$\begin{aligned} \mu_3 &= E[\{X-E(X)\}^3] \\ &= E[X^3-3X^2E(X)+3X\{E(X)\}^2-\{E(X)\}^3] \\ &= E(X^3)-3E(X^2)\,E(X)+3E(X)\{E(X)\}^2-\{E(X)\}^3 \\ &= E(X^3)-3E(X^2)\,E(X)+2\{E(X)\}^3; \end{aligned}$$

similarly for the fourth and higher moments. It will be realised, moreover, that these proofs apply to both discrete and continuous random variables.

18. The variance of the sum (or difference) of two independent random variables is the sum of their variances. This theorem was accepted, without proper proof, in §§114–20 of *Statistics: A Second Edition of a Second Course* after it had been demonstrated numerically. It may now be proved formally as follows.

Let the independent random variables X and Y be measured with their respective means as origins. This implies that

$$E(X) = 0 \quad \text{and} \quad E(Y) = 0$$

and hence
$$\begin{aligned}\text{var}\,(X \pm Y) &= E(X \pm Y)^2 \\ &= E(X^2 \pm 2XY + Y^2) \\ &= E(X^2) \pm 2E(X)\,E(Y) + E(Y^2) \\ &= E(X^2) + E(Y^2) \\ &= \text{var}\,(X) + \text{var}\,(Y).\end{aligned}$$

Further extensions of this theorem are

(i) $\text{var}\,(X_1 + X_2 + \ldots + X_n) = \text{var}\,(X_1) + \text{var}\,(X_2) + \ldots + \text{var}\,(X_n)$

where the n random variables $X_1, X_2, \ldots, X_n$ are independent in pairs; also

(ii)
$$\text{var}(a_1 X_1 + a_2 X_2 + \ldots + a_n X_n) = a_1^2 \text{var}(X_1) + a_2^2 \text{var}(X_2) + \ldots + a_n^2 \text{var}(X_n)$$

where $a_1, a_2, \ldots, a_n$ are constants.

19. The moment generating function. The knowledge of the mean and variance of $(X \pm Y)$ established in §§13–18 may be of little use if we do not also know the probability distribution of $(X \pm Y)$. The example of §25 and the exercises of §26 depend on the fact that if the independent random variables X and Y are respectively *Normal* (μ_1, σ_1^2) and *Normal* (μ_2, σ_2^2) then the random variable $(X \pm Y)$ is *Normal* $(\mu_1 \pm \mu_2, \sigma_1^2 + \sigma_2^2)$. This property of Normal distributions is called their *reproductive property*. Poisson distributions also possess a reproductive property (see §45).

In order to establish the reproductive property of Normal distributions we shall use an important mathematical concept called the *moment generating function*. This concept is not, at first, easy to understand but it should be more readily acceptable after the following digression. Let us think of the way in which logarithms facilitate calculations which would otherwise be tedious. Instead of performing the required arithmetic with the numbers as given, the numbers are *transformed* into their logarithms, a simplified version of the arithmetic is performed with the logarithms and the result is finally transformed back to the original number system. In the same way that logarithms facilitate arithmetical calculations the moment generating function, which we are about to define, facilitates the establishment of statistical theorems.

We begin with the probability density function of a random variable. We transform the probability density function into its moment generating function, we then carry out a simplified deductive process on the moment generating function in order to make our deductions about the original probability density function. This process is valid because it can be proved that for any probability density function there exists one and only one moment generating function. Although the moment generating function will be defined in general terms which apply to both discrete and continuous random variables we shall only pursue its use with the latter because we are particularly interested in the deduction of facts about Normal distributions.

20. Definition of the mgf. The moment generating function $M_X(t)$ of the random variable X is the expectation of e^{tX}. Thus, in symbols,

$$M_X(t) = E(e^{tX})$$

and, if X is a *continuous* random variable with probability density function $f(x)$, then

$$M_X(t) = \int_{-\infty}^{\infty} e^{tx} f(x)\,dx.$$

It is convenient to use the respective abbreviations pdf and mgf for probability density function and moment generating function. The reason for the name *moment generating function* will become apparent in §22.

21. The mgf of the Normal pdf. Suppose that X is *Normal* (μ, σ^2). Its pdf is

$$f(x) = \frac{1}{\sigma\sqrt{(2\pi)}} e^{-\frac{1}{2}(x-\mu)^2/\sigma^2}, \quad \text{all } x.$$

Hence its mgf is

$$M_X(t) = \frac{1}{\sigma\sqrt{(2\pi)}} \int_{-\infty}^{\infty} e^{tx}\, e^{-\frac{1}{2}(x-\mu)^2/\sigma^2}\,dx.$$

Substitute $(x-\mu)/\sigma = u$ or $x = \sigma u + \mu$ and we get

$$\begin{aligned} M_X(t) &= \frac{1}{\sqrt{(2\pi)}} \int_{-\infty}^{\infty} e^{t(\sigma u+\mu)} e^{-\frac{1}{2}u^2}\,du \\ &= e^{t\mu} \frac{1}{\sqrt{(2\pi)}} \int_{-\infty}^{\infty} e^{-\frac{1}{2}(u^2-2\sigma tu)}\,du \\ &= e^{t\mu} \frac{1}{\sqrt{(2\pi)}} \int_{-\infty}^{\infty} e^{-\frac{1}{2}\{(u-\sigma t)^2-\sigma^2t^2\}}\,du \\ &= e^{t\mu+\frac{1}{2}\sigma^2t^2} \frac{1}{\sqrt{(2\pi)}} \int_{-\infty}^{\infty} e^{-\frac{1}{2}(u-\sigma t)^2}\,du. \end{aligned}$$

Finally substitute $u-\sigma t = v$, and we obtain the important result that the mgf of the Normal pdf is

$$\begin{aligned} M_X(t) &= e^{\mu t+\frac{1}{2}\sigma^2t^2} \frac{1}{\sqrt{(2\pi)}} \int_{-\infty}^{\infty} e^{-\frac{1}{2}v^2}\,dv \\ &= e^{\mu t+\frac{1}{2}\sigma^2t^2}, \end{aligned}$$

because the normal pdf integrates to unity.

22. Moments via the mgf.* By the definition of §20

$$M_X(t) = E(e^{tX}) = E\left\{1+(tX)+\frac{(tX)^2}{2!}+\ldots+\frac{(tX)^n}{n!}+\ldots\right\}$$

$$= 1+tE(X)+\frac{t^2}{2!}E(X^2)+\ldots+\frac{t^n}{n!}E(X^n)+\ldots$$

because t is a constant as far as taking the expectation is concerned. (The validity of evaluating the expectation term by term is assumed in this volume.) Continued differentiation with respect to t gives

$$M_X'(t) = E(X)+tE(X^2)+\ldots+\frac{t^{n-1}}{(n-1)!}E(X^n)+\ldots,$$

$$M_X''(t) = E(X^2)+\ldots+\frac{t^{n-2}}{(n-2)!}E(X^n)+\ldots$$

and so on to $\quad M_X^n(t) = E(X^n)+\ldots.$

(The validity of differentiating term by term is assumed in this volume.) Thus by substituting $t = 0$ we obtain

$M_X'(0) = E(X)$, the first moment about zero;

$M_X''(0) = E(X^2)$, the second moment about zero;

and eventually

$M_X^n(0) = E(X^n)$, the nth moment about zero.

The name 'moment generating function' is therefore justified.

Now let us apply this to the *Normal* (μ, σ^2) pdf whose mgf is

$$M_X(t) = e^{\mu t+\frac{1}{2}\sigma^2 t^2}.$$

Continued differentiation with respect to t gives

$$M_X'(t) = (\mu+\sigma^2 t)\, e^{\mu t+\frac{1}{2}\sigma^2 t^2},$$

$$M_X''(t) = \{\sigma^2+(\mu+\sigma^2 t)^2\}\, e^{\mu t+\frac{1}{2}\sigma^2 t^2},$$

$$M_X'''(t) = \{3\sigma^2(\mu+\sigma^2 t)+(\mu+\sigma^2 t)^3\}\, e^{\mu t+\frac{1}{2}\sigma^2 t^2}.$$

Hence $\quad E(X) = M_X'(0) = \mu;$

$$E(X^2) = M_X''(0) = \sigma^2+\mu^2$$

and $\quad E(X^3) = M_X'''(0) = 3\sigma^2\mu+\mu^3.$

From these results, it is easy to deduce by §17 that the second and third moments about the mean are σ^2 and zero respectively. It is left as an exercise for the student to continue the process and obtain $3\sigma^4$ for the fourth moment about the mean.

* Certain conditions must be satisfied before the properties of *finite* sums may be applied to *infinite* sums, as they are in §22, 23. The assumption that these conditions hold is justified but some readers may wish to make it a point for further study (see page 102).

23. The mgf of the sum of two independent random variables is the product of their mgfs.* Suppose that X and Y are independent random variables and that $Z = X+Y$. If the mgfs of X, Y and Z are respectively $M_X(t)$, $M_Y(t)$ and $M_Z(t)$ then

$$\begin{aligned} M_Z(t) &= E(e^{Zt}) = E\{e^{(X+Y)t}\} \\ &= E(e^{Xt}e^{Yt}) = E(e^{Xt})\,E(e^{Yt}) \\ &= M_X(t)\,M_Y(t). \end{aligned}$$

From the above it will be realised that, in general, if $X_1, X_2, \ldots, X_n$ are n independent random variables and $Z = X_1+X_2+\ldots+X_n$ then

$$M_Z(t) = M_{X_1}(t)\,M_{X_2}(t)\ldots M_{X_n}(t).$$

24. The reproductive property of Normal pdfs. If X and Y are independent random variables whose pdfs are *Normal* (μ_1, σ_1^2) and *Normal* (μ_2, σ_2^2) respectively and $Z = X+Y$ then

$$\begin{aligned} M_Z(t) &= M_X(t)\,M_Y(t), \quad \text{by §23}, \\ &= e^{\mu_1 t+\frac{1}{2}\sigma_1^2 t^2} e^{\mu_2 t+\frac{1}{2}\sigma_2^2 t^2}, \quad \text{by §21}, \\ &= e^{(\mu_1+\mu_2)t+\frac{1}{2}(\sigma_1^2+\sigma_2^2)t^2}. \end{aligned}$$

Hence the pdf of Z is *Normal* $(\mu_1+\mu, \sigma_1^2+\sigma_2^2)$. In general this reproductive property extends to the n independent normal variables $X_1, X_2, \ldots, X_n$. Also if Y is *Normal* (μ_2, σ_2^2) then $-Y$ is *Normal* $(-\mu_2, \sigma_2^2)$ and hence $(X-Y)$ is *Normal* $(\mu_1-\mu_2, \sigma_1^2+\sigma_2^2)$.

25. Example. *When the manufacturer's instructions for the use of a certain chemical spray for salad vegetables are followed, the concentration of the chemical in the vegetables is, on a suitable scale, Normally distributed with a mean* 47.5 *and standard deviation* 10. *The concentration above which the spray is fatal to man, is, on the same scale, Normally distributed between individuals with mean* 520 *and standard deviation* 100. *Examine the meaning and the truth of the manufacturer's claim that 'only* 1 *person in* 200000 *has a chance as high as* 1 *in* 1000 *of receiving a fatal dose'.*

If there are no residual effects of the chemical from one salad meal to the next, what is the chance that one meal will cause the death of a given person? [Cambridge]

One person in 200000 is 1/200000 = 0.000005. In order to deal with a probability as small as this it is necessary to refer to the table of *critical cases* of $\Phi(x)$ which follows table 1 of the *Cambridge Elementary Statistical Tables*. To fix this probability into the Normal distribution consider

* See footnote, p. 26.

$1-\Phi(x) = 0.000005$. Then $\Phi(x) = 0.999995$ and from the table of critical cases we deduce that $x > 4.417$. This indicates that for 1 person in 200000 a fatal dose might be below

$$\text{the mean} - 4.417 \times \text{standard deviation} = 520 - 441.7$$
$$= 78.3.$$

The chance of receiving a concentration as high as this from a concentration with mean 47.5 and standard deviation 10 is $1-\Phi(x)$, where

$$x = (78.3 - \text{mean})/\text{standard deviation}$$
$$= 3.08.$$

This chance is 1 in 1000. Thus there is a chance that for 1 person in 200000 the fatal concentration is so low that the probability of that person receiving a fatal dose is 1 in 1000.

		Mean	Variance	Standard deviation
Concentration on salad	x	47.5	100	10
Fatal concentration	y	520.0	10000	100
Difference	$(x-y)$	−472.5	10100	100.5

The above table indicates the method of obtaining the probability that one meal will cause the death of a given person. If a person is selected at random and given a salad selected at random, the person will die if the fatal concentration y for him personally happens to be less than the concentration x on the salad served to him. Thus one meal will cause the death of a given person if the difference $(x-y)$ is positive. The probability of this occurring is

$$1-\Phi(472.5/100.5) = 1-\Phi(4.70).$$

To obtain the numerical value of $\Phi(4.70)$ it is necessary to consult tables more comprehensive than the *Cambridge Elementary Statistical Tables*. On page 116, volume 1 of *Biometrika Tables for Statisticians*, E. S. Pearson and H. O. Hartley, Cambridge University Press, we find that $\Phi(4.70)$ is given as $P(4.70) = 0.9999986992$. Hence the required probability may be stated numerically as 0.0000013 approximately.

26. Exercises.

1. Rods are made of a nominal length of 400 mm but in fact they form a Normal distribution with mean 401 mm and standard deviation 3 mm. Each rod costs 6p to make and may be used immediately if its length lies between 398 and 402 mm. If its length is less than 398 mm the rod is useless but has a scrap value of 1p. If its length exceeds 402 mm, it may be shortened and used at a further cost of 2p. Find the average cost per usuable rod. [A.E.B.]

2. An athlete finds that in the high jump he can clear a height of 1.850 m once in five attempts and a height of 1.700 m nine times out of ten attempts. Assuming the heights he can clear in various jumps form a Normal distribution, estimate the mean and standard deviation of the distribution. Calculate the height the athlete can expect to clear once in one thousand attempts.
[A.E.B.]

3. The heights of the men in Ruritania form a Normal distribution with mean 1887.5 mm and standard deviation 65 mm. The heights of the women in Ruritania are Normally distributed with mean 1825 mm and standard deviation 60 mm. What is the probability that, if a Ruritanian man and woman are taken at random, the woman is taller than the man? [A.E.B.]

4. A variate x_1 is Normally distributed about a mean μ_1 with variance σ_1^2. A second variate x_2, independent of x_1, is Normally distributed about a mean μ_2 with variance σ_2^2. Prove that the difference $(x_1 - x_2)$ between the variates is Normally distributed about a mean $(\mu_1 - \mu_2)$ with variance $(\sigma_1^2 + \sigma_2^2)$.

During the assembly of a mass-produced article, a rod has to be fitted into a hole. Measurement of a large number of components showed that the diameters of rod and hole were Normally distributed with mean and standard deviation as follows:

External diameter of rod: mean 99.7 mm, standard deviation 0.15 mm.

Internal diameter of hole: mean 100.2 mm, standard deviation 0.2 mm.

If components are selected at random for assembly, what proportion of rods will not fit? [Cambridge]

5. The Normal table tabulates the integral

$$\Phi(x) = \frac{1}{\sqrt{(2\pi)}} \int_{-\infty}^{x} e^{-\frac{1}{2}t^2}\, dt.$$

Explain how this table may be used to obtain the proportion of observations of a Normal variable of mean μ and variance σ^2 which lie between two given values a and b.

The heights of boys in a given age group are Normally distributed with mean 1500 mm and standard deviation 50 mm; the heights of girls in the same age group are Normal with mean 1475 mm and standard deviation 45 mm. Determine as accurately as you can the probabilities of differences in height greater than 50 mm between:

(*a*) two boys in the group,

(*b*) two girls in the group,

(*c*) a boy and a girl in the group. [Cambridge]

6. The diameter of a round peg is a Normal variable with mean 14.8 mm and standard deviation 0.1 mm; the diameter of the hole in which the peg is supposed to fit is a Normal variable with mean 15.0 mm and standard deviation 0.1 mm. Pegs and holes are paired at random. What proportion of pairs cannot be assembled because the radius of the peg is greater than that of the hole with which it is paired?

If the hole is more than 0.4 mm larger than the peg, then the peg is so loose that it falls out. What proportion of assembled pairs are too loose to hold together? [Cambridge]

7. A sample of 500 taken at random from a Normal population is found to have a mean 6 and a standard deviation 2.31. Another sample of 800 taken at random from a second Normal distribution has a mean 5 and standard deviation 3.08. Estimate the probability that, if a random selection of one value is taken from each population, the value from the second population will be greater than that from the first. [A.E.B.]

8. If x and y are independent random variables, show that the mean of $x+y$ is the sum of the means of x and y. Find the variance of $x+y$.

Sets of three digits are taken at random from a table of random sampling numbers. Find the mean and variance of the sum of the set. [A.E.B.]

9. Two resistors are both made up by joining ten coils in series, so that the resistance of each resistor is the sum of the resistances of the ten coils. The coils are chosen at random from a population which may be assumed to be Normally distributed with standard deviation 0.1 ohm. Obtain limits within which the difference between the resistances of the two resistors will lie in 95 cases out of 100. [Cambridge]

10. Independent variates x and y have means $\bar{x}$, $\bar{y}$ and variances σ_x^2, σ_y^2 respectively. If a and b are constants, show that $ax+by$ has a mean $a\bar{x}+b\bar{y}$ and variance $a^2\sigma_x^2+b^2\sigma_y^2$.

Rods are made with nominal diameter of 3 mm to fit into holes of a nominal diameter 3.02 mm. In fact, the rods have a mean diameter of 3 mm with standard deviation 0.01 mm, while the holes have a mean diameter 3.02 mm with standard deviation 0.0075 mm. Find the standard deviation of the difference between the diameters of a rod and a hole taken at random. [A.E.B.]

11. The Normal table tabulates the integral

$$\Phi(x) = \frac{1}{\sqrt{(2\pi)}}\int_{-\infty}^{x} e^{-\frac{1}{2}t^2}\,dt.$$

Explain how to use this table to obtain the proportion of observations of a Normal variable of mean μ and variance σ^2 which lie above a given value a

(i) where $a > \mu$,
(ii) where $a < \mu$.

The concentration of a certain preservative in the syrup used in canning pineapple must not exceed 12 parts per million. The syrup is made up in batches with the concentration varying Normally between batches with mean 8 parts per million and standard deviation 1.5 parts per million. What proportion of batches exceed the permitted maximum?

If two batches are mixed (equally by volume) the resultant concentration is the average of the concentrations in the constituent batches. What proportion of such mixed samples exceed the permitted maximum? What proportion fall below 4 parts per million (the level at which preservative action is lost)? [Cambridge]

12. The fluorine content (in parts per million) of water which has passed through a certain filtering plant is a Normal variable with mean 46 p.p.m. and standard deviation 7 p.p.m. It is desired that the fluorine content shall only rarely rise above 58 p.p.m.; evaluate what proportion of the output of the plant does in fact exceed this level.

The output of two identical plants is now mixed; it may be assumed that the fluorine content of the resulting output is the mean of the individual contents. What proportion of the new output exceeds the permitted level?

[Cambridge]

13. For the *Rectangular distribution* given in §6, Ex. 2, show that the mgf is given by

$$M_X(t) = \frac{e^{bt} - e^{at}}{(b-a)\,t}.$$

14. For the *Exponential distribution* given in §6, Ex. 3, show that the mgf is given by

$$M_X(t) = \frac{\lambda}{\lambda - t}, \quad \text{provided } t < \lambda.$$

Hence show that the mean is $1/\lambda$, the variance is $1/\lambda^2$ and the third moment about the mean $2/\lambda^3$.

3

ESTIMATION OF PARAMETERS

27. Sampling variance of the mean. In § 105 of *Statistics: A Second Edition of a Second Course* the frequency distribution of means of samples was investigated numerically. The formal statement and proof of the theorem is as follows.

If random samples of size n are drawn from a population of mean μ and variance σ^2, the sampling distribution of the mean $\bar{X}$ of the samples has μ for its mean and σ^2/n for its variance.

Consider one sample of n values, $X_1, X_2, \ldots, X_n$, drawn from the population. Its mean $\bar{X}$ is given by

$$n\bar{X} = \sum_{r=1}^{n} X_r.$$

If similar samples are drawn repeatedly from the population the distribution of their means has an expectation given by

$$\begin{aligned} E(n\bar{X}) &= E\left\{\sum_{r=1}^{n} X_r\right\} \\ &= \sum_{r=1}^{n} E(X_r) \\ &= \sum_{r=1}^{n} \mu \\ &= n\mu. \end{aligned}$$

Hence $$E(\bar{X}) = \mu.$$

Thus the sampling distribution of the mean $\bar{X}$ has μ for its mean.

Moreover, because the n separate values in the sample are independent, the sampling variance of their sum, $n\bar{X}$, is the sum of the variances of the separate values. But each of the separate values is a sample of *one* from the population and has variance σ^2 and thus

$$\begin{aligned} \operatorname{var}(n\bar{X}) &= \operatorname{var}(X_1 + X_2 + \ldots + X_n) \\ &= \operatorname{var} X_1 + \operatorname{var} X_2 + \ldots + \operatorname{var} X_n \\ &= n\sigma^2. \end{aligned}$$

Hence
$$\operatorname{var}(\bar{X}) = \frac{1}{n^2}(n\sigma^2)$$
$$= \sigma^2/n.$$

Thus the sampling distribution of the mean $\bar{X}$ has σ^2/n for its variance.

This implies, of course, that the standard deviation of the sampling distribution of $\bar{X}$ is $\sigma/\sqrt{n}$.

28. Unbiased estimate. Suppose a random sample is drawn from a population and a *statistic* T is calculated from the sample in order to *estimate* the corresponding *parameter* θ of the population. For one sample only, T will have a particular value but if random samples of the same size are drawn repeatedly, T will take different values $T_1, T_2, \ldots, T_n$, say. Thus T itself is a random variable and its distribution is called its *sampling distribution.* T is valuable as an estimator because of the properties of its sampling distribution. If the population mean of the sampling distribution of T is equal to θ then T is said to be an *unbiased estimate* of θ. In symbols this may be stated:

If $E(T) = \theta$ then T is an unbiased (or unbiassed) estimate of θ.

29. Unbiased estimate of μ. In §27 we considered a sample $X_1, X_2, \ldots, X_n$ and proved that $E(\bar{X}) = \mu$. This indicates that the mean of the sample is an unbiased estimate of the mean of the population.

30. Unbiased estimate of σ². Continuing our study of the sample

$$X_1, X_2, \ldots, X_n$$

with mean $\bar{X}$ let us consider the expectation of the sum of the squares

$$\begin{aligned}
E\left[\sum_{r=1}^{n}(X_r-\bar{X})^2\right] &= E\left[\sum_{r=1}^{n}\{(X_r-\mu)-(\bar{X}-\mu)\}^2\right], \quad \text{where } \mu = E(X) \\
&= E\left[\sum_{r=1}^{n}\{(X_r-\mu)^2-2(X_r-\mu)(\bar{X}-\mu)+(\bar{X}-\mu)^2\}\right] \\
&= E\left[\sum_{r=1}^{n}(X_r-\mu)^2-2(\bar{X}-\mu)\sum_{r=1}^{n}(X_r-\mu)+n(\bar{X}-\mu)^2\right] \\
&= \sum_{r=1}^{n}E[(X_r-\mu)^2]-2E[(\bar{X}-\mu)\,n(\bar{X}-\mu)] \\
&\quad +nE[(\bar{X}-\mu)^2] \\
&= nE[(X_r-\mu)^2]-nE[(\bar{X}-\mu)^2] \\
&= n\operatorname{var}(X)-n\operatorname{var}(\bar{X}) \\
&= n\sigma^2-n(\sigma^2/n), \quad \text{by §27,} \\
&= (n-1)\,\sigma^2.
\end{aligned}$$

Hence $$E\left[\sum_{r=1}^{n}(X_r-\bar{X})^2\Big/(n-1)\right]=\sigma^2.$$

This implies that $$\sum_{r=1}^{n}(X_r-\bar{X})^2$$

must be divided by $(n-1)$, and not n, in order to obtain an unbiased estimate of σ^2.

31. Unbiased estimate of σ. The result obtained in §30 does not imply that

$$\sqrt{\left[\sum_{r=1}^{n}(X_r-\bar{X})^2\Big/(n-1)\right]}$$

is an unbiased estimate of σ. Indeed further investigation shows that it is a biased estimate of σ and that, for Normal populations it should be multiplied by

$$1+\frac{1}{4(n-1)}$$

to obtain an unbiased estimate of σ provided n is not ridiculously small. Thus, if $n = 11$,

$$\sqrt{\left[\sum_{r=1}^{n}(X_r-\bar{X})^2\Big/(n-1)\right]}$$

should be increased by $2\frac{1}{2}\,\%$ to obtain an unbiased estimate of σ but if $n = 26$ it need only be increased by 1 %. A final summary of §§30 and 31 might be as follows.

Although the divisor $(n-1)$ *leads to an unbiased estimate of* σ^2 *it tends to give an under estimate of* σ.

32. Exercises.

1. The discrete variable R takes the values 1, 2, 3, ..., N with respective probabilities $p_1, p_2, p_3, \ldots, p_N$. Interpret the statement

$$\sum_{r=1}^{N} p_r = 1.$$

Define the population mean, μ, and population variance, σ^2, of R and explain how to estimate the parameters from a sample of independent observations $R_1, R_2, \ldots, R_n$.

Prove that your estimate of σ^2 is unbiased. Is the square root of this estimate an unbiased estimate of σ? You may quote the result var $(\bar{R}) = \sigma^2/n$ where

$$\bar{R}=\frac{1}{n}\sum_{i=1}^{n}R_i.$$

[Cambridge]

2. Explain what is meant by an *unbiased estimate*. Show that for a random sample X_i ($i = 1, 2, 3, \ldots, n$) of n observations, with mean $\bar{X}$, an unbiased estimate of the population variance is

$$\frac{1}{(n-1)}\sum_{i=1}^{n}(X_i-\bar{X})^2.$$

Rods are being made with a nominal diameter 5.64 mm. A random sample of ten is measured and found to have diameters

5.613, 5.682, 5.636, 5.671, 5.652, 5.629, 5.677, 5.645, 5.639, 5.668.

Estimate the variance of the population
(i) by the above formula, and
(ii) by using the range.
Find 95 % confidence limits for the population mean. [A.E.B.]

3. Ten observations of the Normal variable X gave $\Sigma X = 14.2$, $\Sigma X^2 = 43.14$. Obtain limits which may be said to enclose μ, the expectation of X, with 95 % confidence. Explain as precisely as you can the phrase 'with 95 % confidence'. [Cambridge]

4. A sample of four taken at random from a population has a mean of 1.6 and the sum of the squares of the deviations from the mean is 9.2. A sample of five is taken at random from the same population and has a mean of 1.8 and a sum of squares of deviations from this mean of 10.1.

Give unbiased estimates of the mean and variance of the population. [A.E.B.]

4

THE BINOMIAL DISTRIBUTION

33. Probability generating function. The ideas already introduced in *Statistics: A Second Edition of a Second Course* are summarised by the following formal theorem.

If the probability of the success of an event at a given trial is p, the probability that there will be exactly r successes in n independent trials is equal to the coefficient of t^r in the expansion in powers of t of $(1-p+pt)^n$. *Also* $E(r) = np$ *and* $\mathrm{var}(r) = np(1-p)$.

If the probability of success is p then the probability of failure is q where $q = 1-p$. In a series of n independent trials the probability that there are exactly r successes and $n-r$ failures in one *specified order* is, by the multiplication rule,

$$p^r q^{n-r}.$$

But the number of *different orders* in which the r successes may occur is the number of ways of choosing r positions from the n possible positions for the successes and that is $\binom{n}{r}$. Hence, by the addition rule, the probability p_r of exactly r successes in the n independent trials is

$$p_r = \binom{n}{r} p^r q^{n-r}$$

and this is the coefficient of t^r in the expansion of

$$(q+pt)^n = (1-p+pt)^n$$

in powers of t.

The function $(1-p+pt)^n$ from which the probability p_r is obtained as the coefficient of t^r is called the *probability generating function* (the pgf) of the Binomial distribution. The pgf of the Poisson distribution is discussed in §42.

Suppose we write

$$(q+pt)^n = p_0+p_1 t+p_2 t^2+\dots+p_n t^n. \tag{1}$$

By putting $t = 1$ we obtain

$$\begin{aligned} \sum_{r=0}^{n} p_r &= (q+p)^n \\ &= 1, \end{aligned}$$

an obvious result because the total probability is unity. Now let us differentiate both sides of (1) with respect to t to obtain

$$np(q+pt)^{n-1} = p_1+2p_2t+\ldots+np_nt^{n-1}. \quad (2)$$

By putting $t = 1$ we obtain

$$np = \sum_{r=0}^{n} rp_r$$
$$= E(r), \quad \text{the expectation of } r.$$

Multiply (2) by t and then differentiate again with respect to t and we obtain

$$np(q+pt)^{n-1}+n(n-1)\,p^2t(q+pt)^{n-2} = 1^2p_1+2^2p_2t+\ldots+n^2p_nt^{n-1}$$

and by putting $t = 1$ $\quad np+n(n-1)\,p^2 = \sum_{r=0}^{n} r^2p_r$

$$= E(r^2).$$

Hence $\quad \operatorname{var}(r) = E(r^2)-\{E(r)\}^2$

$$= np(1-p).$$

34. Examples.

EXAMPLE 1. *In a certain competition for teams of six the qualifying event consists of each member of the team being allowed up to three attempts at a particular trial, the team as a whole qualifying if at least four members of the six succeed in the trial. Assuming that the probability of failure in any one attempt by any member of the team is q, evaluate the probability of the team qualifying.* [Cambridge]

The probability of a member being eliminated is q^3. Hence the probability of a member's success is $(1-q^3)$.

For the team of six members the probability of at least four successes is the sum of the coefficients of t^6, t^5 and t^4 in the expansion of $\{q^3+(1-q^3)t\}^6$.

Thus the probability of the team qualifying is

$$(1-q^3)^6+6(1-q^3)^5\,q^3+15(1-q^3)^4\,q^6 = (1-q^3)^4\,(1+4q^3+10q^6).$$

EXAMPLE 2. *Playing a certain 'one-armed bandit', which is advertised to 'Increase your money tenfold', costs $2\frac{1}{2}p$ a turn; the player is returned 25p if more than 8 balls out of a total of 10 drop in a specified slot. The chance of any one ball dropping is p. Determine the chance of winning in a given turn, and for $p = 0.65$ calculate the mean profit made by the machine on 500 turns.*

Evaluate the proportion of losing turns in which the player comes within one or two balls of winning ($p = 0.65$). [Cambridge]

The probability of more than 8 out of 10 is the sum of the coefficients of t^{10} and t^9 in the expansion of $\{(1-p)+pt\}^{10}$. This is

$$p^{10}+10p^9(1-p) = p^9(10-9p).$$

Thus, when $p = 0.65$, the chance of winning is 0.08594. In 500 turns 25p will be won $500\times 0.08594 = 43$ times. Hence the machine receives £12.50 and pays out £10.75 making a profit of £1.75.

The proportion of losing turns in which the player comes within one or two balls of winning is the sum of the coefficients of t^8 and t^7 in the expansion of $\{(1-p)+pt\}^{10}$. This is

$$45p^8(1-p)^2+120p^7(1-p)^3 = 0.428, \quad \text{when } p = 0.65.$$

Thus on 42.8 % of his turns the player comes within 1 or 2 balls of winning, on 8.6 % of his turns the player actually wins and in the remaining 48.6 % of his turns he loses badly.

EXAMPLE 3. *In lawn tennis a set is won by the first player to win 6 games, except that if the score reaches 5–5 the set is won by the first player to lead by 2 games. Two players have chances respectively p and q of winning in any game* ($p+q = 1$); *games may be treated as independent. Find the chance that a set lasts exactly* $2n+2$ *games* ($n \geqslant 5$). [Cambridge]

This question will be better understood by considering separate special cases.

(i) When $n = 5$. The number of games in this case $2n+2 = 12$. Hence the final score is 7–5. The score 5–5 must appear first and out of the first 10 games each player must win 5. The expansion of $(p+q)^{10}$ gives the probability of this as

$$\frac{10\cdot 9\cdot 8\cdot 7\cdot 6}{1\cdot 2\cdot 3\cdot 4\cdot 5}\,p^5q^5.$$

Following this *either* player p wins the next 2 games and the probability of this is p^2, *or* player q wins the next 2 games and the probability of this is q^2.

Hence the *total* probability of the final score being 7–5 is

$$\frac{10\cdot 9\cdot 8\cdot 7\cdot 6}{1\cdot 2\cdot 3\cdot 4\cdot 5}\,(p^2+q^2)\,p^5q^5.$$

(ii) When $n = 6$. The final score is 8–6. Hence the intermediate scores must be first 5–5, then 6–6, then 8–6. Thus the total probability is

$$\frac{10\cdot 9\cdot 8\cdot 7\cdot 6}{1\cdot 2\cdot 3\cdot 4\cdot 5}\,p^5q^5\,(pq+qp)\,(p^2+q^2) = \frac{10\cdot 9\cdot 8\cdot 7\cdot 6}{1\cdot 2\cdot 3\cdot 4\cdot 5}\,p^5q^5\,(2pq)\,(p^2+q^2).$$

(iii) When $n = 7$.

$$\text{Total probability} = \frac{10\cdot 9\cdot 8\cdot 7\cdot 6}{1\cdot 2\cdot 3\cdot 4\cdot 5}\,p^5q^5\,(2pq)^2\,(p^2+q^2).$$

Thus *in general the total probability* that a set lasts $2n+2$ games ($n \geqslant 5$) is

$$\frac{10\cdot 9\cdot 8\cdot 7\cdot 6}{1\cdot 2\cdot 3\cdot 4\cdot 5}\, p^5q^5(2pq)^{n-5}(p^2+q^2) = \tfrac{63}{8}(2pq)^n\,(p^2+q^2).$$

35. Binomial probabilities via the Normal distribution table. For large samples the calculation of Binomial probabilities becomes tedious because high powers of p and q are involved and the number of terms to be evaluated and summed is large. The Normal distribution is a limiting form of the Binomial distribution as $n \to \infty$. Consequently, by working with mean $\mu = np$ and variance $\sigma^2 = npq$, the Normal distribution table may be used to obtain approximations to the Binomial distribution provided n is sufficiently large. The minimum size of n for which the Normal distribution is a close approximation to the Binomial distribution depends on the value of p. The Normal approximation to the Binomial is quite good provided np and $n(1-p)$ are both greater than 5.

The examples which follow will make these ideas clear and illustrate how they are used.

36. Comparison of the ordinates of a Binomial distribution with those of the corresponding Normal distribution. *Calculate the ordinates of the Binomial distribution given by the coefficients of powers of t in the expansion of* $(\frac{2}{3}+\frac{1}{3}t)^9$ *and draw a frequency polygon showing the result. Find the mean and variance of the distribution.*

Find the ordinates at 0, 1, 2, 3, 4, 5, 6, 7, 8, 9 *of the Normal distribution which has the same mean and variance and draw a frequency polygon with these ordinates.* [A.E.B.]

For the given Binomial distribution $n = 9$, $p = \frac{1}{3}$ and hence the mean $\mu = 3$ and the variance $\sigma^2 = 2$. The Normal distribution which is an approximation to the given Binomial distribution has ordinates given by

$$y = \frac{1}{\sigma\sqrt{(2\pi)}}\, e^{-\frac{1}{2}(r-\mu)^2/\sigma^2}$$

where r takes the discrete values 0, 1, 2, ..., 9. Thus, if $x = (r-\mu)/\sigma$, y can be obtained from table 1 of the *Cambridge Elementary Statistical Tables* by multiplying

$$\phi(x) = \frac{1}{\sqrt{(2\pi)}}\, e^{-\frac{1}{2}x^2}$$

by $1/\sigma$. The numerical requirements of the example are shown in table 4A. The drawing of the frequency polygons is left as an exercise for the reader. Note that, although the value of np is less than the minimum of 5 stated in §35, the Normal distribution is quite a close approximation to the Binomial distribution. Exercises 4, 5, 6, 7 of §41 are further illustrations

TABLE 4A. *Comparison of the ordinates of a Binomial distribution with those of the corresponding Normal distribution*

r	Ordinates of Binomial distribution p_r	$x = (r-\mu)/\sigma$ $= (r-3)/\sqrt{2}$	Ordinates of Normal distribution $\frac{1}{\sigma\sqrt{(2\pi)}} e^{-\frac{1}{2}x^2}$
0	0.026	−2.12	0.030
1	0.117	−1.41	0.104
2	0.234	−0.71	0.219
3	0.273	0.00	0.282
4	0.205	0.71	0.219
5	0.102	1.41	0.104
6	0.034	2.12	0.030
7	0.007	2.83	0.005
8	0.001	3.54	0.001
9	0.001	4.24	0.000

TABLE 4B. *Comparison of the Binomial probabilities with the areas of strips of unit width under the Normal probability curve*

r	Binomial probability p_r	$x = (r-\mu)/\sigma$ $= (r-3)/\sqrt{2}$	$\Phi(x)$	Normal approximation to Binomial probability
$-\frac{1}{2}$		−2.475	0.0067	
0	0.026			0.0319
$\frac{1}{2}$		−1.768	0.0386	
1	0.117			0.1058
$1\frac{1}{2}$		−1.061	0.1444	
2	0.234			0.2175
$2\frac{1}{2}$		−0.354	0.3619	
3	0.273			0.2762
$3\frac{1}{2}$		0.354	0.6381	
4	0.205			0.2175
$4\frac{1}{2}$		1.061	0.8556	
5	0.102			0.1058
$5\frac{1}{2}$		1.768	0.9614	
6	0.034			0.0319
$6\frac{1}{2}$		2.475	0.9933	
7	0.007			0.0060
$7\frac{1}{2}$		3.182	0.9993	
8	0.001			0.00065
$8\frac{1}{2}$		3.889	0.99995	
9	0.001			0.00005
$9\frac{1}{2}$		4.600	1.00000 (5 decimals)	

of the way in which the Binomial distribution tends to the Normal distribution when n is sufficiently large.

37. Comparison of the Binomial probabilities with the areas of strips of unit width under the Normal probability curve. Instead of calculating the *ordinate* of the Normal probability curve at the discrete value r it is possible to obtain an approximation to the Binomial probability p_r by calculating the area of a strip of unit width under the Normal probability curve between ordinates at $(r+\frac{1}{2})$ and $(r-\frac{1}{2})$. The calculation for the Binomial distribution with $n = 9$ and $p = \frac{1}{3}$ is shown in table 4B. This method of working with $(r\pm\frac{1}{2})$ is the *correction for continuity* which is necessary when estimating the probabilities of a discrete random variable from the probability distribution of a continuous random variable. The reader will find it a useful exercise to repeat Ex. 4, 5, 6, 7 of §41 by this method of *areas* after doing them by the method of *ordinates*.

38. Example of the use of the Normal approximation. *A large cargo of lemons has, on the average, one bad lemon in five. Find an approximation to the probability that a random sample of* 100 *will contain* 30 *or more bad lemons.* [A.E.B.]

With $p = \frac{1}{5}$, $q = \frac{4}{5}$, $n = 100$ the Normal distribution whose mean $\mu = np = 20$ and standard deviation $\sigma = \sqrt{(npq)} = 4$ can be used as an approximation to the Binomial distribution p_{30} being the strip between $r_{29\frac{1}{2}}$ and $r_{30\frac{1}{2}}$, as in §37. Hence, after correcting for continuity, the probability of 30 or more is obtained as

$$1-\Phi(x), \quad \text{where} \quad x = (29\tfrac{1}{2}-\mu)/\sigma = 2.375.$$

Thus, the probability that a random sample of 100 will contain 30 or more bad lemons is

$$1-\Phi(2.375) = 0.00877.$$

As this is an approximation let us write it 0.009 which is just less than 1 %.

It will be realised that if the Normal distribution were not used in this example the probability of 30 or more would have to be calculated by

$$1-\{p_0+p_1+p_2+\dots+p_{29}\}$$

for which some other method of approximation might be devised.

39. Examples of significance tests.

EXAMPLE 1. *A pack of cards contains five different patterns in equal numbers. A card is drawn at random. It is then replaced, the cards are shuffled and another is drawn at random. A man claims that he can identify the pattern drawn, more often than once in five, without seeing the card.*

In 100 *drawings, how many times at least must he correctly identify the pattern in order to justify his claim at the* 5 % *level of significance?*

If he claims that he can always identify the pattern drawn, how many cards must he name correctly in order to justify his claim at the 0.1 % *level of significance?* [A.E.B.]

The probability of correct identification by pure chance $p = \frac{1}{5}$ and the probability of wrong identification $q = \frac{4}{5}$. For 100 drawings the mean number of correct identifications $np = 20$ and the standard deviation $\sqrt{(npq)} = 4$. When n is large, as in this case, the Binomial distribution approximates to the Normal distribution.

Hence there is a 90 % probability of correct identifications by pure chance within the limits

$$\begin{aligned} \text{mean} \pm 1.645 \text{ S.D.} &= 20 \pm 1.645 \times 4 \\ &= 20 \pm 6.58. \end{aligned}$$

Thus, if $p = \frac{1}{5}$, the probability of identifying *more* than 26.58 by pure chance is less than 5 %.

Hence, if at least 27 correct identifications are made the claim that $p > \frac{1}{5}$ is justified at the 5 % level.

The probability of identifying, by pure chance, n cards drawn at random is $(\frac{1}{5})^n$ and $(\frac{1}{5})^n < \frac{1}{1000}$ if $n \geqslant 5$. Thus, if the man identifies 5 out of 5 cards correctly, the probability that he has done it by pure chance is less than 0.1 % and his claim is justified at the 0.1 % level of significance.

EXAMPLE 2. *Before a by-election for which there are two candidates A and B, inquiries are made of* 400 *voters chosen at random and it is found that* 208 *of them intend to vote for A. Give* 95 % *confidence limits for the percentage of voters favourable to A at the time of the inquiry.*

If, in fact, 55 % *of the voters were in favour of B, what is the probability that a random sample of* 400 *voters will contain at least as many in favour of A as there are in favour of B?* [A.E.B.]

This example assumes that the total number of electors is very large compared with the sample of 400. The probability of a vote for A is $p = 208/400 = 0.52$. The probability of a vote for B is $q = 0.48$. The mean of the distribution $np = 208$ and the standard deviation

$$\sqrt{(npq)} = 9.992.$$

As n is large and p and q are almost equal the distribution approximates closely to Normal.

Hence we may expect 95 % of the votes for A to be between

$$208 \pm 1.96 \times 9.992 = 208 \pm 19.58 \quad \text{out of } 400.$$

Thus the 95 % confidence limits for the percentage of voters favourable to A are

$$52 \pm 5 = 47 \text{ to } 57.$$

If, in fact, $p = 0.45$ and $q = 0.55$ the mean, $np = 180$ and the standard deviation, $\sqrt{(npq)} = 9.95$. Hence, correcting for continuity,

$$\Phi\left(\frac{199.5-180}{9.95}\right) = \Phi(1.96)$$
$$= 0.9750$$

indicates that the probability of *less* than 200 votes for A is 0.975 or $97\frac{1}{2}\%$.

Thus the probability that a random sample of 400 voters will contain at least as many in favour of A as there are in favour of B is $2\frac{1}{2}\%$.

EXAMPLE 3. *The sex ratio at birth in domestic cattle is approximately* 105 *males to* 100 *females. In a sample of wild cattle* 58 *bull calves were obtained in* 100 *single births. Is this sample sufficient to show at the* 5 % *level of significance that the sex ratio in wild cattle is different from that in domestic cattle?*

In a further sample of 125 *single births,* 76 *bull calves were obtained. What conclusion may be drawn from the two samples together?*

[Cambridge]

For *domestic cattle* the probability of a male $p = 105/205 = 0.5122$ and the probability of a female $q = 100/205 = 0.4878$. The established mean number of males per hundred $np = 51.22$ and the standard deviation $\sqrt{(npq)} = 5$.

For large samples like this with p and q nearly equal the Binomial distribution approximates very closely to the Normal distribution and the number N of wild bull calves in a sample of 100 will differ at the 5 % level of significance from the established sex ratio for domestic cattle if N lies outside the range

$$\text{mean} \pm 1.96 \text{ S.D.} = 51.22 \pm 1.96 \times 5$$
$$= 41.4 \text{ to } 61.0.$$

Thus $N = 58$ out of 100 indicates that the sex ratio in wild cattle does not differ, at the 5 % level of significance, from that in domestic cattle.

For a sample of 225 the established mean is 115.2 and the standard deviation 7.5.

Hence the range

$$\text{mean} \pm 1.96 \text{ S.D. is } 100.5 \text{ to } 129.9.$$

Thus $N = 134$ out of 225 indicates that the sex ratio in wild cattle does differ, at the 5 % level of significance, from that in domestic cattle.

40. A significance test is not certain proof or disproof. *If a grocer claims 'All eggs sold in this shop are fresh', the finding of one bad egg is enough completely to disprove his claim. Why can no certain proof or disproof be obtained if he claims '90 % of eggs sold in this shop are fresh'?*

I believe that in fact only 50 % of the eggs are fresh but I will not dispute the claim unless less than 70 % of a sample are fresh. Determine n so that for any sample of n or more eggs there is more than 0.9 chance of disputing the claim when my belief (50 % fresh) is actually correct. [Cambridge]

The only certain way to prove that at least 90 % of the eggs are fresh is to test the whole 100 %. This, of course, is impossible because we must assume that there is a continuous flow from the producers through the grocer to the public. We must, therefore, rely on some form of sampling.

Assuming that 90 % of the eggs are fresh the probabilities $P(0)$, $P(1)$, $P(2)$, $P(3)$, $P(4)$, $P(x \geqslant 5)$ of 0, 1, 2, 3, 4, 5 or more bad eggs in a random sample of 12 are respectively 0.2821, 0.3761, 0.2298, 0.0851, 0.0213, 0.0473. Thus the probability of finding 5 or more bad eggs in a random sample of 12 is less than 5 %. This implies that the finding of 5 or more bad eggs in a random sample of 12 is evidence at the 5 % level of significance that less than 90 % of the eggs are fresh. But it is no certain proof. The existence of the probabilities as far as $P(12) = (0.1)^{12}$ implies that any number of bad eggs between 0 and 12 is possible even though 90 % are fresh. The greater the number of bad eggs in the sample the stronger the evidence becomes; but it is never a certainty.

If, in fact, only 50 % are fresh, a sample of n will conform to the Binomial distribution with $p = q = \frac{1}{2}$. Thus the number of fresh eggs will be distributed about a mean $\mu = \frac{1}{2}n$ with standard deviation $\sigma = \frac{1}{2}\sqrt{n}$. Moreover, provided n is fairly large, the distribution will be approximately Normal and $\Phi\{(x-\mu)/\sigma\}$ will be the probability of less than x fresh eggs in a sample.

For
$$\Phi\{(x-\mu)/\sigma\} > 0.9,$$
$$(x-\mu)/\sigma > 1.2817,$$
and hence
$$x > \mu + 1.2817\sigma.$$

If also x is 70 % of the sample
$$0.7n > \tfrac{1}{2}n + 1.2817(\tfrac{1}{2}\sqrt{n})$$
which gives
$$n > 10.25.$$

Thus, if n is 11 or more, the chance is more than 0.9 that less than 70 % of a sample are fresh.

IMPORTANT. It is very necessary to check this result because, for such a small value of n, the Normal distribution may not be a good enough approximation to the Binomial distribution. Also the number of fresh eggs in a sample varies *discretely* (its values are integers) whilst the value x above varies *continuously*.

For a sample of 11 eggs, 7 or less fresh eggs is less than 70 %. Using the Binomial distribution itself, the probability of 7 or less fresh eggs in a sample of 11 is

$$1-\{\text{probability of 8 or more}\} = 1-\{1+10+55+165\}/2^{11}$$
$$= 0.89.$$

This indicates that the value, $n = 11$, obtained by using the Normal distribution is not quite high enough. For a sample of 12 eggs, 8 or less fresh eggs is less than 70 % and the probability of 8 or less is

$$1-\{1+12+66+220\}/2^{12} = 0.93.$$

Thus the correct value of n is 12 and we can state finally that *if* 50 % *of the eggs are fresh there is more than* 0.9 *chance of getting less than* 70 % *fresh in a sample of* 12 *or more.*

41. Exercises.

1. A machine produces articles with an average of 20 % which are defective. Find an approximate value for the probability that a sample of 400 items will contain more than 96 which are defective. [Northern]

2. In a certain large town, one person in ten is red-haired. What is the probability that a random sample of twenty will contain at least four red-haired persons?

Find the mean and standard deviation of the number of red-haired persons in a random sample of twenty-five. [A.E.B.]

3. A test consists of 50 questions which can be answered *yes* or *no*. The candidates are told to give an answer to every question whether they know the correct answer or are merely guessing. What is the probability that a candidate without any knowledge of the correct answers will get thirty or more right?

Another candidate knows the answers to ten of the questions and answers them correctly but guesses the answers to the other forty. What is the probability that he will get 25 or fewer correct answers? [A.E.B.]

4. Calculate the ordinates at 0, 1, 2, 3, 4, 5, 6, 7, 8, 9, 10, 11, 12 of

(i) the Binomial distribution given by the coefficients of powers of t in the expansion of $(\frac{2}{3}+\frac{1}{3}t)^{18}$, and

(ii) the Normal distribution which has the same mean and variance as the Binomial distribution.

5. Calculate the ordinates at 6, 8, 10, 12, of

(i) the Binomial distribution given by the coefficients of powers of t in the expansion of $(\frac{2}{3}+\frac{1}{3}t)^{36}$ and

(ii) the Normal distribution which has the same mean and variance as the Binomial distribution.

6. Calculate the ordinates at 2, 4, 6, 8, 10, 12, 14 of

(i) the Binomial distribution given by the coefficients of powers of t in the expansion of $(\frac{1}{2}+\frac{1}{2}t)^{16}$ and

(ii) the Normal distribution which has the same mean and variance as the Binomial distribution.

7. Calculate the ordinates at 0, 1, 2, 3, 4, 5, 6, 7, 8, 9, 10 of

(i) the Binomial distribution given by the coefficients of powers of t in the expansion of $(\frac{4}{5}+\frac{1}{5}t)^{25}$ and

(ii) the Normal distribution which has the same mean and variance as the Binomial distribution.

8. Long experience in the use of a certain rat poison has shown that the percentage kill under natural conditions is 47. Laboratory tests with a new poison gave 27 deaths among 43 rats. Test whether this showed a significant improvement over the standard poison, stating the level of significance.

The new poison was then tested under natural conditions and gave 75 deaths among 148 rats. Test whether the laboratory and field results with this poison are compatible. [Cambridge]

9. In an investigation of preferences between pre-packed and fresh cut bacon, 69 housewives preferred pre-packed and 52 preferred fresh cut. Does this result provide evidence (at the 5 % level of significance) of a difference inacceptability?

Find those values of the percentage of housewives preferring pre-packed which could just be regarded as reasonable, that is which just do not differ from the observed proportion at the 5 % level of significance. [Cambridge]

10. If hens of a certain breed lay eggs on four days a week, on the average, find on how many days during a season of 200 days a poultry keeper with eight hens of this breed will expect to receive at least six eggs.

If in fact he received at least six eggs on 42 days during the season of 200 days, would this evidence suggest that any factor other than chance was operating? [Cambridge]

11. The variable x is observed n times, giving values

$$x_1, x_2, \ldots, x_n.$$

State formulae relating the mean and variance of

$$X = a_1x_1+a_2x_2+\ldots+a_nx_n$$

to the mean and variance of x and to the constants $a_1, a_2, \ldots, a_n$.

In throwing a coin a head is scored 1 and a tail 0. Calculate the mean and variance of the score for a single throw of a biased penny, which has a chance p of showing a head.

Hence obtain the mean and variance of the number of successes in n independent trials with constant chance of success p. [Cambridge]

12. At a seed-testing station it is found that a proportion 0.4 of a certain type of seed is fertile. By accident the remaining stock of this seed (whose total amount is very large) is completely mixed with an equal quantity of a second type of seed which is believed to be completely infertile. If this latter assumption is true, what is the probability that a seed taken at random from the mixture will germinate?

Each of seven pots is planted with two seeds taken at random from the mixture. Six pots eventually produce one or more plants each. Is this result consistent, at the 5 % level of significance, with the infertility postulated for the second type of seed? [Cambridge]

13. Obtain the mean and variance of a variable which conforms to a Binomial distribution.

Two such variables r_1 and r_2 are based respectively on n_1 and n_2 trials with chances of success p_1 and p_2. By considering the means and variances of r_1 and r_2, or otherwise, show that r_1+r_2 is Binomial (with n_1+n_2 trials) if and only if $p_1 = p_2$. [Cambridge]

14. In a certain examination the candidates are divided into 4 classes on the written papers and those in the top 3 classes are interviewed. After the interview the candidates are classified A, B or C, the C class including those placed in the fourth class on the written papers. The chance of a candidate obtaining class i ($i = 1, 2, 3, 4$) on the written paper is p_i, and the chance of his then being finally classified as A, B, C is p_{ia}, p_{ib}, p_{ic} ($i = 1, 2, 3$); thus p_{2c} is the chance of a candidate who has been placed in the second class on the written papers being finally classified as C, so that $p_{2a}+p_{2b}+p_{2c} = 1$. Write down the chance

(*a*) that of 8 given candidates at least 6 will be interviewed;
(*b*) that a candidate chosen at random will finish in (i) class A, (ii) class C;
(*c*) that of 4 given candidates none will finish in class A. [Cambridge]

5

POISSON AND EXPONENTIAL DISTRIBUTIONS

42. Probability generating function. If R is a discrete random variable which assumes the values 0, 1, 2, ..., r, ... with probabilities $p_0, p_1, p_2, ..., p_r, ...$ such that

$$p_r = \frac{e^{-a}a^r}{r!},$$

we say that R has a Poisson distribution with parameter $a > 0$. The probability generating function (pgf) in which the probability of R is the coefficient of t^r is

$$e^{-a}\left(1+at+\frac{a^2}{2!}t^2+...+\frac{a^r}{r!}t^r+...\right) = e^{-a}e^{at}.$$

If it is written $\quad p_0+p_1t+p_2t^2+...+p_rt^r+... = e^{a(t-1)},$ (1)

by putting $t = 1$ we confirm that

$$p_0+p_1+p_2+...+p_r+... = 1.$$

By differentiating (1) with respect to t we get

$$p_1+2p_2t+3p_3t^2+...+rp_rt^{r-1}+... = ae^{a(t-1)}, \tag{2}$$

and by putting $t = 1$ we obtain

$$\sum_{r=0}^{\infty} rp_r = a.$$

Thus the expected value of R $\quad E(R) = a.$

Multiplying (2) by t we get

$$tp_1+2p_2t^2+3p_3t^3+...+rp_rt^r+... = ate^{a(t-1)},$$

from which, by differentiating with respect to t, we obtain

$$p_1+2^2p_2t+3^2p_3t^2+...+r^2p_rt^r+... = ae^{a(t-1)}+a^2te^{a(t-1)}. \tag{3}$$

By putting $t = 1$ in (3) we get

$$\sum_{r=0}^{\infty} r^2p_r = a+a^2.$$

Thus $\quad E(R^2) = a+a^2$

and
$$\operatorname{var}(R) = E(R^2)-\{E(R)\}^2$$
$$= a.$$

Hence the mean and the variance of the Poisson distribution are both equal to a.

43. General discussion of the pgf. Paragraphs 33 and 42 illustrate the elegance of the pgf when dealing with the Binomial and Poisson distributions. In general, if the discrete random variable R takes the values $0, 1, 2, \ldots, r, \ldots$ with respective probabilities $p_0, p_1, p_2, \ldots, p_r, \ldots$, we may write the *pgf* as

$$P(t) = p_0+p_1 t+p_2 t^2+\ldots+p_r t^r+\ldots$$
$$= \sum_{r=0}^{\infty} p_r t^r.$$

Then
$$P(1) = p_0+p_1+p_2+\ldots+p_r+\ldots$$
$$= \sum_{r=0}^{\infty} p_r$$
$$= 1, \quad \text{the total probability.}$$

By differentiating $P(t)$ with respect to t and then substituting $t = 1$ we get

$$P'(1) = 0p_0+1p_1+2p_2+\ldots+rp_r+\ldots$$
$$= \sum_{r=0}^{\infty} rp_r$$
$$= E(R), \quad \text{the expectation of } R.$$

By differentiating $tP'(t) = 1p_1 t+2p_2 t^2+\ldots+rp_r t^r+\ldots$ with respect to t and then putting $t = 1$ we get

$$P''(1)+P'(1) = \sum_{r=0}^{\infty} r^2 p_r$$
$$= E(R^2).$$

Thus the variance of R is given by

$$\operatorname{var}(R) = E(R^2)-\{E(R)\}^2$$
$$= P''(1)+P'(1)-\{P'(1)\}^2.$$

44. The pgf of the sum of two independent discrete random variables. Suppose two independent discrete random variables X and Y have respective pgfs

$$P(t) = p_0+p_1 t+p_2 t^2+\ldots+p_x t^x+\ldots$$
$$Q(t) = q_0+q_1 t+q_2 t^2+\ldots+q_y t^y+\ldots.$$

We require the probability that the sum of X and Y will take the value r. Now the probability that X will have the value s and at the same time Y will have the value $r-s$ is the product of probabilities $p_s q_{r-s}$ and, summing for all the possible values of s from 0 to r, we see that the total probability that $(X+Y)$ will have the value r is

$$p_0 q_r + p_1 q_{r-1} + p_2 q_{r-2} + \ldots + p_r q_0 = \sum_{s=0}^{r} p_s q_{r-s}.$$

But this is the coefficient of t^r in the product $P(t)\,Q(t)$. Hence the pgf of the sum $(X+Y)$ of the two independent discrete random variables X and Y is the product of their separate pgfs.

45. The reproductive property of Poisson distributions. If $P(t)$ and $Q(t)$ are the pgfs of two independent Poisson variables, X and Y with respective means a_1 and a_2 then

$$P(t) = e^{a_1(t-1)} \quad \text{and} \quad Q(t) = e^{a_2(t-1)}.$$

Now, by §44, the pgf of the sum $(X+Y)$ is

$$P(t)\,Q(t) = e^{(a_1+a_2)(t-1)}$$

and this is the pgf of a Poisson variable with mean (a_1+a_2). Thus the sum of two independent Poisson variables with means a_1 and a_2 is a Poisson variable with mean (a_1+a_2).

The exercise which follows summarises a simple traffic survey which was made to verify this theorem.

46. Exercise.

(*a*) *The arrival rate of Southbound vehicles*

Number of cars per 30-second interval	0	1	2	3	4	5	6 or more	Total
Number of intervals	18	32	28	20	13	9	0	120

(*b*) *The arrival rate of Northbound vehicles*

Number of cars per 30-second interval	0	1	2	3	4	5	6	7 or more	Total
Number of intervals	9	16	30	22	19	10	14	0	120

(*c*) *The arrival rate of Southbound and Northbound combined*

Number of cars per 20-second interval	0–2	3	4	5	6	7	8	9 or more	Total
Number of intervals	14	19	20	16	19	10	13	9	120

Tables (*a*) (*b*) and (*c*) above are the results of observations made during a period of one hour to verify the theorem of §45. Show by means of χ^2 tests that (*a*), (*b*) and (*c*) are all Poisson distributions and that the mean of distribution (*c*) is equal to the sum of the means of distributions (*a*) and (*b*). (*Note.* The use of χ^2 for testing a Poisson distribution is described in §87, page 73, of *A Second Course in Statistics.*)

47. Approximation of Poisson probabilities by Normal distribution table. Table 5A gives the Poisson probabilities $p_0, p_1, \ldots, p_8$ when $a = 4$ and shows, also, the method of calculating the areas of the corresponding unit strips under the Normal probability curve. Although the Normal

TABLE 5A. *Poisson probabilities when $a = 4$ compared with Normal probabilities*

r	Poisson probability p_r	$x = (r-a)/\sqrt{a}$ $= (r-4)/2$	$\Phi(x)$	Normal probability corresponding to the Poisson probability
$-\frac{1}{2}$		-2.25	0.0122	
0	0.0183			0.0279
$\frac{1}{2}$		-1.75	0.0401	
1	0.0732			0.0655
$1\frac{1}{2}$		-1.25	0.1056	
2	0.1464			0.1210
$2\frac{1}{2}$		-0.75	0.2266	
3	0.1952			0.1747
$3\frac{1}{2}$		-0.25	0.4013	
4	0.1952			0.1974
$4\frac{1}{2}$		0.25	0.5987	
5	0.1562			0.1747
$5\frac{1}{2}$		0.75	0.7734	
6	0.1041			0.1210
$6\frac{1}{2}$		1.25	0.8944	
7	0.0595			0.0655
$7\frac{1}{2}$		1.75	0.9599	
8	0.0297			0.0279
$8\frac{1}{2}$		2.25	0.9878	

probabilities differ slightly from the Poisson they can be accepted as rough approximations. Moreover it should be noted that the Poisson probability

$$P(1 \leqslant r \leqslant 7) = 0.0732+0.1464+\ldots+0.0595,$$
$$= 0.9298,$$

and that the corresponding Normal probability given by

$$\Phi(1.75)-\Phi(-1.75) = 0.9599-0.0401$$
$$= 0.9198.$$

Thus the Normal probability is a good approximation and is much more easily calculated. In other words, if the average number of bad eggs per crate is 4, the probability that the number of bad eggs in any crate is outside the limits 1 to 7 can be estimated quite accurately by using Normal tables instead of the Poisson distribution.

If $a > 4$ the agreement between the probabilities is closer. The reader will find it a useful exercise to make out a table similar to table 5A for $r = 4, 5, ..., 14$ when $a = 9$. It will be found that $P(6 \leqslant r \leqslant 12) = 0.761$ and that the corresponding Normal probability is 0.757.

48. The Exponential distribution. It must be clearly understood that the Poisson probabilities only exist for the discrete values $0, 1, 2, ..., r, ...$ of the variate and that they only apply to *independent events* of *low probability* which have repeated opportunities of *random occurrence.* Poisson probabilities are used in quality control because the proportion of defectives is small, the defectives occur randomly throughout the production and the samples drawn are reasonably large. Accidents also fulfill the necessary conditions and so does traffic on the highway provided it flows freely and the vehicles do not arrive too frequently. Another traffic problem of the same type is that of demands on a telephone route. In this case the calls come independently from a large number of subscribers at random intervals. Suppose the mean number of calls per unit time is λ. It follows that the probability of a call arriving in any small interval of time δt is $\lambda\,\delta t$ and from this we can deduce the probability distribution of the time interval between calls. Consider the following example.

Telephone calls arrive at a switchboard independently and at random, the probability of a call arriving in any interval δt being $\lambda\,\delta t$. Obtain:

(*a*) *the chance that no calls arrive in the time interval* $(0, T)$ *after the operator comes on duty;*

(*b*) *the chance that a call arrives in the interval* $(T, T+\delta T)$ *after the preceding call;*

(*c*) *the mean time between calls;*

(*d*) *the chance that r calls arrive in the interval* $(0, T)$. [Cambridge]

The probability that no call arrives in any interval δt is

$$(1-\lambda\,\delta t).$$

Suppose that the time interval T is divided into n small intervals each of length $T/n = \delta t$. The probability that no calls arrive in any of these small intervals is

$$(1-\lambda\,\delta t)^n = \left(1-\frac{\lambda T}{n}\right)^n$$

which tends to $e^{-\lambda T}$ as $\delta t \to 0$ and $n \to \infty$.

Hence (*a*) the chance that no calls arrive in the time interval $(0, T)$ after the operator comes on duty is $e^{-\lambda T}$.

Also (*b*) the chance that a call arrives in the interval $(T, T+\delta T)$ after the preceding call is the chance that no calls arrive in the interval $(0, T)$ but that one does arrive in the following interval δT and that is $e^{-\lambda T}\lambda\,\delta T$. This implies that the time interval between consecutive calls has a probability distribution given by

$$\mathrm{d}p = \lambda \mathrm{e}^{-\lambda T}\,\mathrm{d}T.$$

Thus the time interval t between consecutive calls has a probability density function $y = \lambda \mathrm{e}^{-\lambda t}$, and (*c*) the mean time between calls is

$$\begin{aligned}\int_0^\infty t\lambda \mathrm{e}^{-\lambda t}\,\mathrm{d}t &= [-t\mathrm{e}^{-\lambda t}]_0^\infty + \int_0^\infty \mathrm{e}^{-\lambda t}\,\mathrm{d}t \\ &= 0 + [-\mathrm{e}^{-\lambda t}/\lambda]_0^\infty \\ &= 1/\lambda.\end{aligned}$$

Then (*d*) the chance that r calls arrive in the interval $(0, T)$ is the chance that there are calls in any r of the n intervals δt but no calls in the remaining $(n-r)$ intervals δt. This is

$$\begin{aligned}\binom{n}{r}(\lambda\,\delta t)^r(1-\lambda\,\delta t)^{n-r} &= \frac{n(n-1)\,\dots\,(n-r+1)}{r!}\left(\frac{\lambda T}{n}\right)^r\left(1-\frac{\lambda T}{n}\right)^{n-r} \\ &= \frac{1(1-1/n)\,\dots\,(1-(r-1)/n)}{r!}(\lambda T)^r\frac{(1-\lambda T/n)^n}{(1-\lambda T/n)^r}\end{aligned}$$

which tends to $\mathrm{e}^{-\lambda T}(\lambda T)^r/r!$ as $n \to \infty$ while r remains constant. It is convenient to reserve the name *Poisson distribution* for the distribution of discrete probabilities

$$r^{-a},\ a\mathrm{e}^{-a},\ \frac{a^2}{2!}\mathrm{e}^{-a},\ \dots,\ \frac{a^r}{r!}\mathrm{e}^{-a},\ \dots$$

and to call the continuous probability distribution

$$\mathrm{d}p = \lambda \mathrm{e}^{-\lambda t}\,\mathrm{d}t$$

the *Poissonian law of traffic incidence* or the *Exponential distribution.*

FINAL SUMMARY. *If incidents occur according to the Poissonian law with an average of λ incidents per unit time then the time interval between incidents has a probability distribution*

$$dp = \lambda e^{-\lambda t}\,dt$$

the mean time between incidents being $1/\lambda$.

49. The distribution of the sum of two time intervals. *The chance that a single customer in a certain shop completes service in the interval $(t, t+\delta t)$ after commencing service is $\lambda\,\delta t$. Show that the frequency function of service time is $\lambda e^{-\lambda t}$ and find the mean service time.*

If two customers arrive together and are served by a single assistant, obtain the frequency function of the sum of their service times and also the mean of this sum.

$$\left[\textit{You may assume that } \lim_{n\to\infty}\left(1+\frac{x}{n}\right)^n = e^x.\right]$$ [Cambridge]

The first part of this example is the same as parts (*a*), (*b*), (*c*) of §48, the *serving of a customer* being substituted for the *arrival of a call.*

If two customers arrive together and are served by one assistant, suppose that the service of the second customer is completed in the interval $(t+\delta t,\ t+2\delta t)$. Also, suppose as before that the interval t is divided into n small intervals each of length $t/n = \delta t$. The service of the second customer must be completed in the *last interval* δt and, before then, there are *n intervals* δt in which no service is completed and *one interval* δt in which the service of the first customer is completed. The *one interval* δt may occur in any one of the $(n+1)$ time spaces indicated thus $*$ in the following probability expression:

$$*\,(1-\lambda\delta t)*(1-\lambda\delta t)*\ldots*(1-\lambda\delta t)*\lambda\delta t.$$

Hence the *total* probability that both will have been served by the time $t+2\delta t$ has elapsed is

$$\begin{aligned}\delta p &= (n+1)\,(1-\lambda\delta t)^n\,(\lambda\delta t)^2\\ &= \lambda^2\left(1-\frac{\lambda t}{n}\right)^n\{(n+1)\delta t\}\delta t\\ &= \lambda^2\left(1-\frac{\lambda t}{n}\right)^n\{t+\delta t\}\delta t.\end{aligned}$$

Thus, when $n\to\infty$ and $\delta t\to 0$, we have

$$\mathrm{d}p = \lambda^2 t\mathrm{e}^{-\lambda t}\mathrm{d}t,$$

which implies that the probability density function of the total service time for two customers is $y = \lambda^2 t\mathrm{e}^{-\lambda t}$.

The mean of this total service time is then

$$\int_0^\infty t\{\lambda^2 t\mathrm{e}^{-\lambda t}\}\mathrm{d}t = 2/\lambda,$$

using the method of integration by parts. This result, that the mean service time for two customers is twice the mean time for one customer, is what one would intuitively expect.

50. Examples of significance and maximum likelihood.

EXAMPLE 1. *The probability P_r that there will be r damaged tomatoes in a crate can be taken as*

$$P_r = \frac{e^{-m}m^r}{r!},$$

where m is the expectation of r. Over a large number of crates the value of m has been found to be 10. *In the first crate from a new supplier the value of r was* 4. *Test whether this is significant evidence that the value of m for this supplier is less than* 10; *explain carefully the logic of your argument.*

[Cambridge]

Based on the null hypothesis that the expectation of r is 10 the *total* probability of obtaining a value of r *as small as* 4 in any sample is

$$P_0+P_1+P_2+P_3+P_4 = \mathrm{e}^{-10}\{1+10+50+166\tfrac{2}{3}+416\tfrac{2}{3}\}$$
$$= 0.029$$

which is less than 5 % (but greater than $2\frac{1}{2}$ %). The evidence that the value of m for the new supplier is less than 10 is, therefore, significant at the 5 % level. (The evidence is not significant at the $2\frac{1}{2}$ % level but the 5 % level is the usually accepted *arbitrary* level.)

EXAMPLE 2. *The variable r follows a Poisson distribution, so that*

$$P_r = \frac{e^{-m}m^r}{r!};$$

the mean of r is m and its standard deviation is $m^{\frac{1}{2}}$. *In repeated observations the values* r_1, r_2 *and* r_3 *were obtained. Write down the joint probability of these observations; this expression is known as the* likelihood *of the sample. Obtain as a function of* r_1, r_2, r_3 *the value* $\hat{m}$ *of m which makes this likelihood a maximum.*

Show that the mean of $\hat{m}$ *is m and find its standard deviation.*

[Cambridge]

The joint probability of the observations r_1, r_2, r_3 is

$$P_{r_1}P_{r_2}P_{r_3} = \frac{\mathrm{e}^{-3m}\,m^{(r_1+r_2+r_3)}}{r_1!\,r_2!\,r_3!},$$

known as the *likelihood* of the sample. To maximise this let L denote the natural logarithm of the likelihood; then

$$L = -3m+(r_1+r_2+r_3)\ln m-(\ln r_1!+\ln r_2!+\ln r_3!)$$

and $$\frac{\mathrm{d}L}{\mathrm{d}m} = -3+\frac{1}{m}(r_1+r_2+r_3) = 0$$

when $$m = \tfrac{1}{3}(r_1+r_2+r_3).$$

Moreover $\mathrm{d}^2L/\mathrm{d}m^2 = -(r_1+r_2+r_3)/m^2$, being negative, shows that the value $\hat{m}$ of m which makes the likelihood a maximum is

$$\hat{m} = \tfrac{1}{3}(r_1+r_2+r_3).$$

Also the mean of

$$\begin{aligned}(r_1+r_2+r_3) &= \text{mean } r_1+\text{mean } r_2+\text{mean } r_3\\ &= m+m+m\\ &= 3m\end{aligned}$$

and hence the mean of

$$\begin{aligned}\hat{m} &= \text{mean of } \tfrac{1}{3}(r_1+r_2+r_3)\\ &= m.\end{aligned}$$

This may be expressed in symbols as

$$\begin{aligned}E(\hat{m}) &= E\{\tfrac{1}{3}(r_1+r_2+r_3)\}\\ &= \tfrac{1}{3}E(r_1+r_2+r_3)\\ &= \tfrac{1}{3}3E(r)\\ &= E(r)\\ &= m.\end{aligned}$$

It implies, of course, that $\hat{m}$ is an unbiased estimate of m if m is unknown.

Continuing with

$$\begin{aligned}\operatorname{var}(r_1+r_2+r_3) &= \operatorname{var} r_1+\operatorname{var} r_2+\operatorname{var} r_3\\ &= 3m,\end{aligned}$$

we obtain the variance of

$$\begin{aligned}\tfrac{1}{3}(r_1+r_2+r_3) &= \tfrac{1}{9}(3m)\\ &= \tfrac{1}{3}m.\end{aligned}$$

Hence the standard deviation of $\hat{m} = (\frac{1}{3}m)^{\frac{1}{2}}$.

Note 1. It is often useful to take logarithms before differentiating to find a maximum in the likelihood function.

Note 2. In this investigation there is only one stationary point. But, a non-negative function vanishing at $\pm\infty$ (which a pdf must be) must have a finite maximum. Therefore the *one* stationary point *must* be a maximum. Thus the investigation of the second derivative was unnecessary. This idea might save considerable time in a more complicated example.

51. Exercises.

1. In a large factory the number of accidents reported each day gave the following distribution for 100 days:

Number of accidents reported	0	1	2	3	4
Number of days	56	30	10	3	1

Compare the figures with a Poisson distribution having the same mean. State whether there is any evidence against the hypothesis that the accidents occur independently. [A.E.B.]

2. In a town, over nine years, the number of suicides per month gave the following distribution:

Number of suicides	x	0	1	2	3
Number of months	f	61	41	5	1

Calculate the frequencies of the Poisson distribution having the same mean and total frequency. Is there any evidence that the suicides do not occur independently? [A.E.B.]

3. The distribution of accidents on the M1 motorway, during the first year after it was opened, for the 355 days when conditions were normal (no bad ice, snow, fog, etc.).

Number of accidents in a day	0	1	2	3	4	5	6 or more
Number of days	116	113	77	36	8	5	0

Show, by means of a χ^2 test, that the accidents conform to a Poisson distribution.

4. An airline finds that, on the average, 4 % of the persons who reserve seats for a certain flight do not, in fact, turn up for the flight. Consequently, the airline decides to allow 75 persons to reserve seats on a plane which can accommodate only 73 passengers. What is the probability that there will be a seat available for every person who turns up for the flight? [Northern]

5. The telephone calls received by a switchboard conform to a Poisson distribution with a mean of 3 calls per minute. Find the probability that in a given minute there will be five or more calls.

If the duration of every call is three minutes and at most ten calls can be connected simultaneously, find an approximation to the probability that, at a given instant, the switchboard is fully loaded.

6. The following table shows the results of recording the telephone calls handled at a village telephone exchange between 1 p.m. and 2 p.m. on each of 100 weekdays (e.g. on 36 days no such calls were made):

Calls	0	1	2	3	4 or more
Days	36	35	22	7	0

Assuming that calls arrive independently and at random, estimate

(i) the mean m of the corresponding Poisson probability distribution;

(ii) the probability that if the operator is absent for 10 minutes no call will be missed;

(iii) the probability that if the operator is absent for 10 minutes *two or more* calls will be missed. [Cambridge]

7. The number of bacteria in 1 ml of inoculum may be assumed to follow a Poisson distribution with mean 2. Assuming further that at least 3 bacteria are needed for a dose to be infective, calculate the probability that out of 10 doses each of 1 ml, exactly 4 will produce infection. [Cambridge]

8. An innoculum contains an average of 5 bacteria per ml. What are the chances that

(*a*) a 1 ml sample contains no bacteria;

(*b*) a 2 ml sample contains less than 4 bacteria?

Culture specimens are prepared with 1 ml samples of the innoculum; a specimen will not grow if it contains less than 2 bacteria. What is the value of the probability that out of five cultures exactly four will grow? [Cambridge]

9. *The prediction of future arrivals of vehicles.* Because the traffic along a certain road was heavy (over 400 vehicles per hour) doubts were raised as to whether or not the Poisson distribution should be used to predict future arrivals. The following table summarises the results of observations taken during a busy period:

Number of vehicles per half minute	0	1	2	3	4	5	6	7	8 or more
Observed frequency	0	9	6	9	11	9	5	1	0

(i) Show, by calculation, that the variance is approximately equal to the mean. This suggests that the distribution is approximately Poisson.

(ii) Carry out a χ^2 test to show that the arrival of vehicles conforms to the Poissonian law.

(iii) What is the probability of more than 2 minutes elapsing between arrivals?

10. *An extract from a Ministry of Transport traffic flow table.*

Traffic flow vehicles per hour	Number of gaps per hour exceeding		
	7 seconds	10 seconds	15 seconds
600	186	114	48
750	172	98	30
900	156	74	21
1000	140	50	16

Suppose the traffic flow at a certain place is 900 vehicles per hour. Use the Poissonian law to estimate the probability of more than 10 seconds elapsing between consecutive vehicles. Hence obtain the number of 10-second traffic-free gaps to be expected in any hour thus verifying the figure 74 given in the above table. Verify similarly the other figures given in the table.

11. *Probability of finding a vacant space at a parking meter* (2 p.m.–4 p.m. on Mondays to Fridays).

Number of vacant spaces	0	1	2	3	4	5 or more
Number of occasions	29	42	21	16	12	0

The above observations were obtained for the meter parking spaces in a certain street by first dividing the 10-hour observation period, 2 p.m.–4 p.m. on Mondays to Fridays, into 120 5-minute intervals. During each 5-minute interval one observation was made; the exact time of it within each interval was randomised. Each observation consisted of an instantaneous count of the number of vacant spaces. Show that the distribution does not differ significantly from a Poisson distribution. Hence estimate the probability of finding *one or more* vacant spaces at any instant between 2 p.m. and 4 p.m. on Mondays to Fridays.

12. At a certain road intersection the number of vehicles 'turning right' was observed during each of 300 3-minute intervals. The intervals were randomly distributed throughout various hours of the day and various days of the week. The observations are summarised in the following table:

Number of vehicles turning right in the 3-minute interval	0	1	2	3	4	5	6	7	8	9	10 or more
Number of intervals	14	30	36	68	43	43	30	14	10	12	0

Show that the distribution differs significantly from a Poisson distribution and state the level of significance. What does this imply?

13. *Occurrence of vacant spaces in a car park.* On a busy day, over a period of six hours, the spaces in a car park were re-taken immediately after being vacated. For each 3-minute interval of the six hours the number of spaces vacated was recorded and the results of the investigation are summarised in the following frequency distribution:

Number of spaces vacated during the 3-minute intervals	x	0	1	2	3	4	5	6	7 or more	Total
Number of intervals	f	17	37	27	24	10	4	1	0	120

(i) Show that the mean of the distribution, correct to 2 decimal places, is 1.91 and that the variance is approximately equal to the mean.

(ii) Carry out a χ^2-test to show that the occurrence of vacant spaces conforms to the Poissonian law. Hence show that the probability of waiting more than 5 minutes for a space is less than 5 %.

(iii) If the vacating of spaces becomes less frequent, to what value may the mean of the distribution fall before the probability of waiting more than 5 minutes becomes greater than 5 %?

14. In a manufacturing process, on the average one article in twenty is defective. Use the Poisson distribution to estimate the probability that a box of 100 articles will contain

(*a*) no defective article,

(*b*) fewer than three defectives.

A random sample of 20 of the articles is found to contain three defectives. Is it likely that, on the average, only one article in 20 is defective?

[A.E.B.]

15. A variable r follows a Poisson distribution with unknown mean m. In a sample of n observations the values 0, 1, 2, ..., of r occur with frequencies $f_0, f_1, f_2, \ldots$; $\Sigma f_i = n$. Write down the joint probability of this sample and determine the value, $\hat{m}$, of m which maximises the joint probability (this is the *maximum likelihood estimate* of m).

Show that $\hat{m}$ is an unbiased estimate of m and find its variance.

[Cambridge]

6

EXAMPLES AND EXERCISES INDICATING THE WAY AHEAD

52. Change of variable examples.

EXAMPLE 1. *A point P is taken at random on a line OA of unit length and a square is described on OP. This square has an area of y square units. Find the mean and variance of y.* [A.E.B.]

Method (i). Let $OP = x$ so that the area, y, of the square on OP is

$$y = x^2.$$

As x varies from 0 to 1 it follows that y varies from 0 to 1 by a one-to-one transformation. Moreover, because P is taken at random on OA it follows that x varies *uniformly* between 0 and 1. This means that its probability distribution function is

$$f(x) = 1, \quad \text{if } 0 \leqslant x \leqslant 1,$$
$$f(x) = 0, \quad \text{otherwise.}$$

Thus the probability, $\mathrm{d}p$, that x lies in the interval of width $\mathrm{d}x$ between $x-\frac{1}{2}\mathrm{d}x$ and $x+\frac{1}{2}\mathrm{d}x$ is given by

$$\mathrm{d}p = \mathrm{d}x.$$

But since $x = y^{\frac{1}{2}}$ it follows that

$$\mathrm{d}x = \tfrac{1}{2}y^{-\frac{1}{2}}\mathrm{d}y$$

and hence $$\mathrm{d}p = \tfrac{1}{2}y^{-\frac{1}{2}}\mathrm{d}y.$$

This indicates that the probability density function of y is

$$g(y) = \tfrac{1}{2}y^{-\frac{1}{2}}, \quad \text{if } 0 \leqslant y \leqslant 1,$$

and $$g(y) = 0, \quad \text{otherwise.}$$

Thus $$E(y) = \int_0^1 yg(y)\mathrm{d}y = \tfrac{1}{3},$$

and $$\operatorname{var}(y) = E(y^2)-\{E(y)\}^2 = \tfrac{4}{45}.$$

Method (ii). The total area under the probability curve of x

$$\int_0^1 \mathrm{d}x = 1$$

is *transformed* by the substitution $x = y^{\frac{1}{2}}$ to

$$\int_0^1 \tfrac{1}{2}y^{-\frac{1}{2}}\,\mathrm{d}y = 1$$

and hence y is distributed between 0 and 1 with probability density $\frac{1}{2}y^{-\frac{1}{2}}$. The results $E(y) = \frac{1}{3}$ and var $(y) = \frac{4}{45}$ then follow as before.

EXAMPLE 2. *A sector of a circle of unit radius and angle θ, is cut from sheet metal and bent to form the curved surface of a right circular cone of height x. If, for a large number of such sectors, the angle θ is rectangularly distributed between* 0 *and* 2π, *show that x is distributed between* 0 *and* 1 *with a probability distribution*

$$p(x)\,dx = \frac{x}{\sqrt{(1-x^2)}}\,dx.$$

Sketch the probability curve and calculate the median and quartiles.

[Northern]

The relation between the height, x, of the cone and the angle, θ, of the sector is

$$x^2+(\theta/2\pi)^2 = 1.$$

As θ is rectangularly distributed between 0 and 2π the total area under its probability curve is

$$\int_0^{2\pi} \frac{1}{2\pi}\,\mathrm{d}\theta = 1,$$

and by the substitution $\theta = 2\pi(1-x^2)^{\frac{1}{2}}$

this is transformed to $$\int_0^1 \frac{x}{\sqrt{(1-x^2)}}\,\mathrm{d}x = 1.$$

Thus x is distributed between 0 and 1 with a probability distribution

$$p(x)\mathrm{d}x = \frac{x}{\sqrt{(1-x^2)}}\,\mathrm{d}x.$$

The median or 50th percentile, p_{50}, is given by

$$\int_0^{p_{50}} \frac{x}{\sqrt{(1-x^2)}}\,\mathrm{d}x = 0.5.$$

This gives $p_{50} = \sqrt{3}/2$. The *lower quartile*, p_{25}, is given by

$$\int_0^{p_{25}} \frac{x}{\sqrt{(1-x^2)}}\,\mathrm{d}x = 0.25,$$

and the *upper quartile*, p_{75}, is given by

$$\int_0^{p_{75}} \frac{x}{\sqrt{(1-x^2)}}\,dx = 0.75.$$

These give $p_{25} = \sqrt{7}/4$ and $p_{75} = \sqrt{15}/4$.

The drawing of the curve $f(x) = x/\sqrt{(1-x^2)}$ is left as an exercise for the reader.

53. Exercises.

1. The length x of the side of a square is rectangularly distributed between 1 and 2. Show that the area y of the square is distributed between 1 and 4 with a probability distribution $p(y)\,dy = \frac{1}{2}y^{-\frac{1}{2}}\,dy$.

Sketch the frequency curve, and calculate the mean and variance of the area of the square.

2. The length x of the edge of a cube is rectangularly distributed between 5 and 10. Show that the volume y of the cube is distributed between 125 and 1000 with a probability distribution $p(y)\,dy = \frac{1}{15}y^{-\frac{2}{3}}\,dy$.

Sketch the frequency curve, and calculate the mean and variance of the volume of the cube. [Northern]

3. The radius x of a circle is rectangularly distributed between 1 and 2. Show that the area y of the circle is distributed between π and 4π with probability distribution

$$p(y)\,dy = \tfrac{1}{2}\pi^{-\frac{1}{2}}y^{-\frac{1}{2}}\,dy.$$

Sketch the probability curve and calculate the mean and the variance of the area of the circle. [Northern]

4. The two equal sides of an isosceles triangle are each of unit length and the angle θ between them is rectangularly distributed between 0 and $\frac{1}{6}\pi$. Show that the area y of the triangle is distributed between 0 and $\frac{1}{4}$ with probability distribution

$$p(y)\,dy = \frac{12}{\pi}(1-4y^2)^{-\frac{1}{2}}\,dy.$$

Sketch the probability curve and calculate the mean and variance of the area of the triangle. [Northern]

54. Transformation of median and percentiles. The following example emphasises the important fact that, in a transformation, the median of the new distribution can be obtained by transforming the median of the old distribution. This also applies to any percentile but it does not apply to the mean.

A mass-produced circular disc should have radius 2 *cm but in fact the values of the radius are uniformly distributed in the range* 1.95–2.10 *cm.*

Explain why

(*a*) *median of the area* $= \pi$ (*median of the radius*)^2,

(*b*) *mean of the area* $\neq \pi$ (*mean of the radius*)^2.

Obtain limits A_L *and* A_U *for the area such that* 20 % *of the discs have area* $< A_L$ *and* 20 % *have area* $> A_U$. [Cambridge]

As the radius, x cm, is uniformly distributed between 1.95 and 2.10 cm the area under its probability curve is

$$\int_{1.95}^{2.10} \frac{1}{0.15}\,dx = 1.$$

The median of the radius is the value of x which bisects the area under the probability curve. Thus the median, R_M, of the radius is given by

$$\int_{1.95}^{R_M} \frac{1}{0.15}\,dx = \tfrac{1}{2},$$

from which it is easy to deduce that $R_M = 2.025$ cm.

If y cm^2 is the area of a disc then $y = \pi x^2$ and, by substituting $x = y^{\frac{1}{2}}\pi^{-\frac{1}{2}}$ in the area under the probability curve for x we obtain

$$\int_{\pi(1.95)^2}^{\pi(2.10)^2} \frac{1}{0.30}\,y^{-\frac{1}{2}}\pi^{-\frac{1}{2}}\,dy = 1$$

as the area under the probability curve for y.

Suppose the same substitution is made in

$$\int_{1.95}^{R_M} \frac{1}{0.15}\,dx = \tfrac{1}{2},$$

we shall obtain
$$\int_{\pi(1.95)^2}^{A_M} \frac{1}{0.30}\,y^{-\frac{1}{2}}\pi^{-\frac{1}{2}}\,dy = \tfrac{1}{2}$$

where $A_M = \pi R_M{}^2$ and A_M is the median of the area. Thus we may state that

(*a*) median of the area $= \pi$ (median of radius)^2.

If 1.95 and 2.10 are replaced by R_1 and R_2 respectively, the mean of the area

$$\bar{y} = \int_{\pi R_1^2}^{\pi R_2^2} \frac{1}{2(R_2-R_1)}\,y^{\frac{1}{2}}\pi^{-\frac{1}{2}}\,dy$$
$$= \tfrac{1}{3}\pi(R_2{}^2+R_2R_1+R_1{}^2).$$

But the mean of the radius $= \frac{1}{2}(R_2+R_1)$ and hence

(*b*) the mean of the area $\neq \pi$ (mean of radius)^2.

Note that the general values R_1 and R_2 were introduced in this case because, when $R_1 = 1.95$ and $R_2 = 2.10$, the reader will find that the numerical value of $\frac{1}{3}(R_2{}^2+R_2R_1+R_1{}^2)$ is approximately equal to $\frac{1}{4}(R_2+R_1)^2$. This renders the argument with the numerical values rather unconvincing.

The statement (*a*) can be extended by transforming

$$\int_{1.95}^{R_L} \frac{1}{0.15}\,\mathrm{d}x = \tfrac{1}{5} \quad \text{to} \quad \int_{\pi(1.95)^2}^{A_L} \frac{1}{0.30}\,y^{-\frac{1}{2}}\pi^{-\frac{1}{2}}\,\mathrm{d}y = \tfrac{1}{5}.$$

This indicates that the 20th percentile of the area, A_L, can be derived from the 20th percentile of the radius R_L by

$$A_L = \pi R_L^{\,2}.$$

Now R_L is easily evaluated as 1.98 cm and hence $A_L = 12.32\ \text{cm}^2$. Similarly $A_U = \pi R_U^{\,2}$ where

$$\int_{1.92}^{R_U} \frac{1}{0.15}\,\mathrm{d}x = \tfrac{4}{5}.$$

Hence $R_U = 2.07$ cm and $A_U = 13.46\ \text{cm}^2$.

55. Examples of the use of Taylor's theorem in approximations of the mean and variance. The following two examples illustrate the use of Taylor's theorem in obtaining approximations for the mean and variance of a variable which results from a transformation.

EXAMPLE 1. *A variable x has mean m and small variance v; a variable y is a known function of x, f(x). By considering the expansion of f(m+h), or otherwise, show that*

$$\text{mean } (y) \simeq f(m) + \tfrac{1}{2}vf''(m).$$

The radius of a mass-produced circular disc is uniformly distributed in the range 1.95–2.10 *cm. By using the above formula or otherwise, find the approximate mean of the area of the disc.* [Cambridge]

EXAMPLE 2. *The random variable x has mean m and small variance v. Show that the variance of the function f(x) is approximately* $v[f'(m)]^2$, *where* $f'(x)$ *is the derivative of f(x); state the order of the terms neglected in this approximation.*

In the manufacture of seconds pendulums, the length l may be assumed to be a Normal variable with mean l_0 *and standard deviation* $0.002l_0$, *where* l_0 *is such that* $T\,[= 2\sigma\sqrt{(l/g)}]$ *is equal to* 2 *when* $l = l_0$. *Obtain limits within which* 95 % *of the periods T will lie.* [Cambridge]

SOLUTION OF 1. The variable x has mean m and small variance v. The substitution $x = m+h$ produces a new variable h with mean zero and small variance v. This implies that, although h may vary from $-\infty$ to $+\infty$, the probability of it taking anything but small values is negligible.

We may, therefore, suppose that h is distributed in the small interval (h_1, h_2) with probability function $p(h)$, and that

$$\int_{h_1}^{h_2} p(h)\,\mathrm{d}h = 1, \quad \int_{h_1}^{h_2} hp(h)\,\mathrm{d}h = 0, \quad \int_{h_1}^{h_2} h^2 p(h)\,\mathrm{d}h = v.$$

Now
$$y = f(m+h)$$
$$\simeq f(m)+hf'(m)+\tfrac{1}{2}h^2f''(m),$$

using Taylor's expansion and neglecting higher powers of h because h is small. Thus y is a function of h and the probability that h falls in the interval of width $\mathrm{d}h$ between $h-\frac{1}{2}\mathrm{d}h$ and $h+\frac{1}{2}\mathrm{d}h$ is $p(h)\mathrm{d}h$. Hence

$$\begin{aligned}\text{mean}\,(y) &\simeq \int_{h_1}^{h_2} p(h)\,\{f(m)+hf'(m)+\tfrac{1}{2}h^2f''(m)\}\,\mathrm{d}h\\ &\simeq f(m)\int_{h_1}^{h_2} p(h)\,\mathrm{d}h+f'(m)\int_{h_1}^{h} hp(h)\,\mathrm{d}h+\tfrac{1}{2}f''(m)\int_{h_1}^{h_2} h^2p(h)\,\mathrm{d}h\\ &\simeq f(m)+\tfrac{1}{2}vf''(m).\end{aligned}$$

If x is uniformly distributed in the range 1.95–2.10 cm, m = 2.025 cm and v = 0.001875 cm^2. Also $y = \pi x^2$ implies $f(x) = \pi x^2$ and $f''(x) = 2\pi$ and hence mean $(y) = 4.1025\pi$.

SOLUTION OF 2. This example is a continuation of the previous example. Proceeding with

$$\text{var}\,y \simeq \int_{h_1}^{h_2} p(h)\,\{f(m)+hf'(m)+\tfrac{1}{2}h^2f''(m)\}^2\,\mathrm{d}h-[\text{mean}\,(y)]^2,$$

by neglecting powers of h *higher than* h^2 we obtain

$$\begin{aligned}\text{var}\,y &\simeq \int_{h_1}^{h_2} p(h)\,\{[f(m)]^2+2hf(m)f'(m)+h^2f(m)f''(m)+h^2[f'(m)]^2\}\,\mathrm{d}h\\ &\qquad\qquad -[\text{mean}\,(y)]^2\\ &\simeq \{[f(m)]^2+vf(m)f''(m)+v[f'(m)]^2\}-[f(m)+\tfrac{1}{2}vf''(m)]^2\\ &\simeq v[f'(m)]^2,\end{aligned}$$

since the term containing v^2 must be neglected because v itself is of the same order as h^2.

If the length, l, of the seconds pendulum is Normally distributed, since $T^2 = 4\pi^2l/g$, it follows that T^2 varies directly as l and, therefore, T^2 is Normally distributed and the 95 % limits for T^2 can be obtained as

$$\text{mean}\,(T^2) \pm 1.96 \text{ standard deviation}\,(T^2).$$

Supposing that $f(l) = T^2 = 4\pi^2l/g$

then $f'(l) = 4\pi^2/g$

and $f''(l) = 0.$

Hence $\text{mean}\,(T^2) \simeq f(l_0)+\tfrac{1}{2}vf''(l_0),$

by example 1 above, $\simeq \dfrac{4\pi^2l_0}{g},$

$\simeq 4,$

because it is given that $2\pi\sqrt{(l_0/g)} = 2.$

Also
$$\text{var}(T^2) \simeq v[f'(l_0)]^2$$
$$\simeq (0.002l_0)^2\,[4\pi^2/g]^2$$
$$\simeq (0.002)^2\,[4]^2$$

and hence
$$\text{standard deviation}\,(T^2) \simeq 0.008.$$

Thus the limits within which 95 % of the values of T^2 will lie are

$$4 \pm 1.96 \times 0.008 = 4(1 \pm 3.92 \times 10^{-3})$$

which implies that 95 % of the periods T will lie within the limits

$$2(1 \pm 3.92 \times 10^{-3})^{\frac{1}{2}}.$$

56. Minimum variance example. *The number of hits, r, registered by a Geiger counter in time T may be assumed to have both mean and variance equal to λT where λ is a constant depending on the strength of the source. A source is observed for times T_1 and T_2 and independent counts r_1 and r_2 are obtained. Show how to choose weights ω_1 and ω_2 so that $l = \omega_1 r_1 + \omega_2 r_2$ has mean λ and variance as small as possible.*

Suggest the extension of your result to the case of three independent observations of the source, and determine the variance of l in this case.

[Cambridge]

If
$$E(l) = E(\omega_1 r_1 + \omega_2 r_2)$$
$$= \omega_1 E(r_1) + \omega_2 E(r_2)$$
$$= \omega_1 \lambda T_1 + \omega_2 \lambda T_2$$
$$= \lambda,$$

then
$$\omega_1 T_1 + \omega_2 T_2 = 1. \tag{1}$$

Also
$$\text{var}(l) = \text{var}(\omega_1 r_1 + \omega_2 r_2)$$
$$= \omega_1^2\,\text{var}(r_1) + \omega_2^2\,\text{var}(r_2)$$
$$= \omega_1^2 \lambda T_1 + \omega_2^2 \lambda T_2$$
$$= \lambda\{\omega_1^2 T_1 + (1-\omega_1 T_1)^2/T_2\} \quad \text{by (1) above}$$
$$= \frac{\lambda T_1}{T_2}\left\{\omega_1^2(T_1+T_2) - 2\omega_1 + \frac{1}{T_1}\right\}. \tag{2}$$

Hence
$$\frac{\mathrm{d}}{\mathrm{d}\omega_1}\text{var}(l) = \frac{2\lambda T_1}{T_2}\{\omega_1(T_1+T_2) - 1\}$$
$$= 0 \quad \text{when } \omega_1 = 1/(T_1+T_2).$$

Also $\mathrm{d}^2\,\text{var}(l)/\mathrm{d}\omega_1^2$ is positive. Moreover when $\omega_1 = 1/(T_1+T_2)$ we find, by (1) above, that $\omega_2 = 1/(T_1+T_2)$ also. Thus l has mean λ and minimum variance when

$$\omega_1 = \omega_2 = 1/(T_1+T_2)$$

and by substituting this value of ω_1 in (2) above we find that the minimum variance is $\lambda/(T_1+T_2)$.

The corresponding results for the case of three independent observations are:

$$\omega_1 = \omega_2 = \omega_3 = 1/(T_1+T_2+T_3)$$

and

$$\text{minimum variance} = \lambda/(T_1+T_2+T_3).$$

An alternative method of determining the minimum variance is to express (2) above in the form

$$\text{var (l)} = \frac{\lambda T_1(T_1+T_2)}{T_2}\left\{\left(\omega_1-\frac{1}{T_1+T_2}\right)^2+\frac{T_2}{T_1(T_1+T_2)^2}\right\}$$

by 'completing the square'.

This indicates that the minimum variance is $\lambda/(T_1+T_2)$ when

$$\omega_1 = 1/(T_1+T_2).$$

57. Exercises.

1. Give the conditions under which the number, r, of successes in n trials will have a Binomial distribution.

In sets of n_1, n_2 independent trials, all with the same chance, p, of success, the number of successes were r_1, r_2. Obtain constants a_1 and a_2 so that the expression $a_1r_1+a_2r_2$ has expectation p and variance as small as possible.

[Cambridge]

2. Independent observations x_1, x_2 are taken of the variable x, which has expectation θ. Obtain constants a_1, a_2 so that

$$X = a_1x_1+a_2x_2$$

has expectation θ and variance as small as possible. State the generalisation of this estimate to the case of more than two observations.

Five observations of x gave average 3.6 with estimated variance (of the average) 1.5; a further seven observations gave average 6.0 with estimated variance (of the average) 1.0. Estimate the expectation of x and give the estimated variance of your estimate. [Cambridge]

58. Probability and level of significance example. *Show that the probability of needing exactly r independent trials to achieve k successes, when the chance of success in each trial is p, is*

$$\binom{r-1}{k-1} p^k q^{r-k}, \quad \textit{where } q = 1-p.$$

In a certain training programme there are 3 *tests; attempts at these tests can be regarded as independent trials and experience has shown that a candidate's chance of success at any trial is* 0.5. *Calculate the probability of a candidate needing a total of less than* 5 *attempts to pass all* 3 *tests.*

Explain how, if a candidate needed 4 attempts, you would use this probability in a test of the null hypothesis that he was no better than average.

[Cambridge]

The probability of needing exactly r independent trials to achieve k successes is the probability of obtaining $(k-1)$ successes in $(r-1)$ trials followed by a success in the rth trial. This is

$$\left[\binom{r-1}{k-1} p^{k-1}q^{(r-1)-(k-1)}\right]\times[p] = \binom{r-1}{k-1} p^k q^{r-k}.$$

The probability of needing a total of less than 5 attempts is the sum of the probabilities of needing 3 and 4 attempts. This is

$$p^3+\binom{3}{2} p^3 q = \tfrac{1}{8}+\tfrac{3}{16} = \tfrac{5}{16}.$$

Asssuming that the candidate is *average*, his chance of success in any trial is 0.5 and the chance of him needing 4 attempts *or less* to pass all three tests is $\frac{5}{16}$ or $31\frac{1}{4}$ %. This is the *level of significance* of his performance above the average. As it is much greater than 5 % his performance must be regarded as no better than average.

Suppose on the other hand that average chance of success at any trial had been 0.2. Then the probability of a candidate needing 4 attempts or less would be $17/625 = 2.72$ %. In this case, therefore, if a candidate needed 4 attempts to pass he could be regarded as better than average at the 5 % level of significance but not at the $2\frac{1}{2}$ % level.

In the next section we see that the number of attempts taken by candidates to pass all three tests is a discrete random variable, R, whose value may be any positive integer greater than 2 and whose *probability generating function* is

$$P(t) = p^3t^3(1-qt)^{-3}.$$

It is an example of a *negative Binomial distribution.*

59. Normal approximation example. *As an extension of the last example obtain the expectation and variance of the number of attempts, R, taken by candidates to pass all three tests. Find also the mode of the distribution.*

If X is a Normal variable with the same mean and variance as R find $P(X < 4\frac{1}{2})$ *and compare it with* $P(R \leqslant 4)$.

The number of attempts, R, is the discrete random variable

$$R = 3, 4, 5, 6, \ldots$$

with probability distribution

$$p_r = p^3, \binom{3}{2} p^3q, \binom{4}{2} p^3q^2, \binom{5}{2} p^3q^3, \ldots$$
$$= p^3\{1, 3q, 6q^2, 10q^3, \ldots\}.$$

Note that $$p^3\{1+3q+6q^2+10q^3+\ldots\} = 1$$

and that $$1+3q+6q^2+10q^3+\ldots = p^{-3} = (1-q)^{-3}$$

and also that the *probability generating function* of R is

$$P(t) \equiv p^3t^3(1-qt)^{-3} = p_3t^3+p_4t^4+p_5t^5+p_6t^6+\ldots$$

where p_r is the coefficient of t^r (see §43). Hence

$$P'(t) = 3p^3t^2(1-qt)^{-3}+3p^3t^3(1-qt)^{-4}q$$

and $$P''(t) = 6p^3t(1-qt)^{-3}+18p^3t^2(1-qt)^{-4}q+12p^3t^3(1-qt)^{-5}q^2.$$

Thus
$$\begin{aligned} E(R) &= P'(1) \\ &= 3p^3(1-q)^{-3}+3p^3(1-q)^{-4}q \\ &= 3+3(q/p), \quad \text{because } 1-q = p, \\ &= 6 \quad \text{when } p = \tfrac{1}{2}; \end{aligned}$$

also
$$\begin{aligned} \text{var}\,(R) &= P''(1)+P'(1)-\{P'(1)\}^2 \\ &= 6 \quad \text{also when } p = \tfrac{1}{2}. \end{aligned}$$

When $p = q = \frac{1}{2}$ the numerical values of $p_3, p_4, p_5, p_6, \ldots$ are $\frac{1}{8}, \frac{3}{16}, \frac{3}{16}, \frac{5}{32}, \ldots$ from which we see that the modal values of R are 4 and 5. That is to say the most frequent number of attempts needed to pass all three tests is 4 or 5.

If X is a Normal variable with $\mu = 6$ and $\sigma^2 = 6$ then

$$\begin{aligned} P(X < 4\tfrac{1}{2}) &= 1-\Phi\{(6-4\tfrac{1}{2})/\sqrt{6}\} \\ &= 0.27 \quad \text{by tables.} \end{aligned}$$

Thus the Normal distribution (when the necessary correction for continuity is made) gives a fairly good approximation to $P(R \leqslant 4) = 0.3125$ obtained in the last example.

60. Mean and variance of rounding error in computation. *In constructing four-figure tables, entries are calculated to five figures and rounded according to the following rule. A typical five-digit decimal fraction* $0.123jk$ *is rounded to* $0.123j$ *if* $k = 0, 1, 2, 3, 4$ *and to* $0.123(j+1)$ *if* $k = 6, 7, 8, 9$; *if* $k = 5$ *it is rounded to* $0.123j$ *if* j *is even and to* $0.123(j+1)$ *if* j *is odd. The rounding error is defined as*

$$\textit{the integer} = (\textit{true entry minus rounded entry}) \times 10^5.$$

Calculate the mean and standard deviation of the rounding error.

[Cambridge]

It seems reasonable to assume that the values 0, 1, 2, ..., 9 are equally probable for both the digits j and k. Thus the probability of each value of

k is $\frac{1}{10}$ and the probability of $k = 5$ with j even is $\frac{1}{20}$ and of $k = 5$ with j odd is $\frac{1}{20}$. The following tabulated calculation is self-explanatory.

$$E(x) = \Sigma x P(x) = 0.$$

$$\text{var}(x) = \Sigma x^2 P(x) = 8.5.$$

$$\sigma = 2.915.$$

k	True entry a	Rounded entry b	Rounding error $x = (a-b)\,10^5$	Probability $P(x)$
0	$0.123j0$	$0.123j$	0	$\frac{1}{10}$
1	$0.123j1$	$0.123j$	1	$\frac{1}{10}$
2	$0.123j2$	$0.123j$	2	$\frac{1}{10}$
3	$0.123j3$	$0.123j$	3	$\frac{1}{10}$
4	$0.123j4$	$0.123j$	4	$\frac{1}{10}$
5 (j even)	$0.123j5$	$0.123j$	5	$\frac{1}{20}$
5 (j odd)	$0.123j5$	$0.123(j+1)$	-5	$\frac{1}{20}$
6	$0.123j6$	$0.123(j+1)$	-4	$\frac{1}{10}$
7	$0.123j7$	$0.123(j+1)$	-3	$\frac{1}{10}$
8	$0.123j8$	$0.123(j+1)$	-2	$\frac{1}{10}$
9	$0.123j9$	$0.123(j+1)$	-1	$\frac{1}{10}$

61. Interval estimate example. *The variable X is uniformly distributed in $(a, a+2)$. Obtain limits (x_1, x_2) such that*

$$P(X \leqslant x_1) = P(X \geqslant x_2) = 0.025.$$

The variable is observed once, the value being x_0. Give a method of obtaining an interval estimate for a which you expect to be correct in 95 % of trials.

Indicate briefly what procedure you would use to obtain such an interval estimate after observing several values of X. [Cambridge]

The shaded areas in fig. 1 represent

$$P(X \leqslant x_1) = P(X \geqslant x_2) = 0.025.$$

Thus $$\tfrac{1}{2}(x_1-a) = \tfrac{1}{2}(a+2-x_2) = 0.025$$

which gives the interval $(x_1, x_2) = (a+0.05, a+1.95)$. The probability that the single observation x_0 lies in the range (a, x_1) is $2\frac{1}{2}$ % if $x_1 = a+0.05$. In this case, therefore, $x_0-a \leqslant 0.05$ or $a \geqslant x_0-0.05$. Thus

$$P(a \geqslant x_0-0.05) = 2\tfrac{1}{2}\,\%.$$

Also, the probability that x_0 lies in $(a+1.95, a+2)$ is $2\frac{1}{2}$ %. In this case

$$a+2-x_0 \leqslant 0.05 \quad \text{or} \quad a \leqslant x_0-1.95.$$

Thus $$P(a \leqslant x_0-1.95) = 2\tfrac{1}{2}\,\%.$$

Hence $$P(x_0-1.95 \leqslant a \leqslant x_0-0.05) = 95\,\%$$

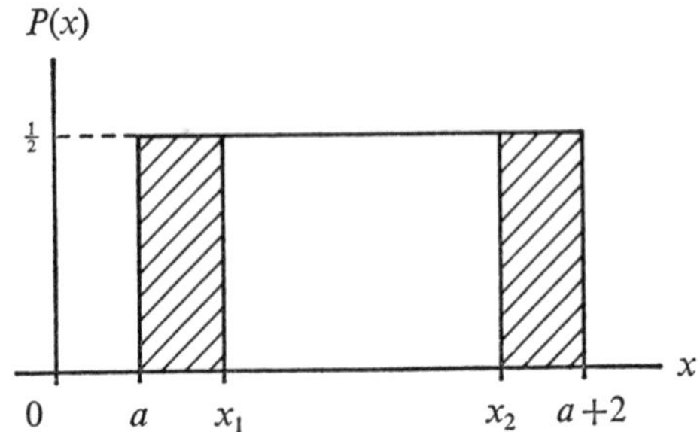

Fig. 1. Variable X uniformly distributed in $(a, a+2)$.

and $(x_0-1.95, x_0-0.05)$ is an *interval estimate* for a which we may expect to be correct in 95 % of trials.

For the given probability distribution

$$E(x) = \int_a^{a+2} \tfrac{1}{2}x\,\mathrm{d}x = a+1$$

and
$$\operatorname{var}(X) = \int_a^{a+2} \tfrac{1}{2}x^2\,\mathrm{d}x-(a+1)^2 = \tfrac{1}{3}.$$

Suppose n values of X are observed and that their mean is $\bar{X}$. Then

$$E(\bar{X}) = a+1 \quad \text{and} \quad \operatorname{var}(\bar{X}) = \frac{1}{3n}.$$

Moreover we may assume $\bar{X}$ is Normally distributed (Central limit theorem). Thus

$$P\{a+1-1.96(3n)^{-\frac{1}{2}} \leqslant \bar{X} \leqslant a+1+1.96(3n)^{-\frac{1}{2}}\} = 95\,\%,$$

and hence

$$P\{\bar{X}-1-1.96(3n)^{-\frac{1}{2}} \leqslant a \leqslant \bar{X}-1+1.96(3n)^{-\frac{1}{2}}\} = 95\,\%.$$

The interval estimate for a,

$$\{\bar{X}-1-1.96(3n)^{-\frac{1}{2}}, \bar{X}-1+1.96(3n)^{-\frac{1}{2}}\},$$

may, therefore, be accepted with 95 % confidence.

62. Four examples of two-dimensional random variables.

EXAMPLE 1. *The variable x is uniformly distributed in* $(0, b)$; *two observations, x_1 and x_2 are taken. Show that all possible pairs of observations can be represented graphically by distinct points in a square. Hence or otherwise show that the probability that* (x_2-x_1) *lies in* $(0, Y)$, *where* $0 \leqslant Y \leqslant b$, *is*

$$P(0 \leqslant x_2-x_1 \leqslant Y) = \frac{1}{2}\left[1-\frac{(b-Y)^2}{b^2}\right].$$

Hence obtain the frequency function of $|x_2-x_1|$.

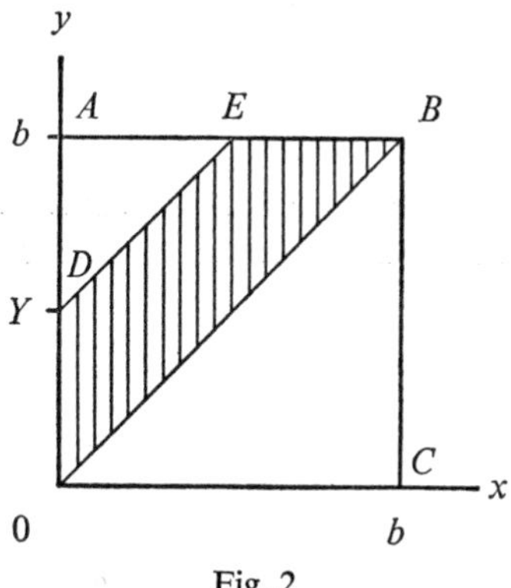

Fig. 2

If b is unknown, by considering the mean of $|x_2 - x_1|$, *or otherwise, obtain an unbiased estimate of b.* [Cambridge]

The statement 'the variable x is uniformly distributed in $(0, b)$' means that x can take any value between 0 and b with equal probability. If two observations x_1 and x_2 are taken, x_1 can be represented between 0 and b along the x-axis and x_2 can be represented between 0 and b along the y-axis. As x_1 and x_2 are independent, for a given x_1 the value of x_2 may be anywhere between 0 and b and for a given x_2 the value of x_1 may be anywhere between 0 and b. All the possible pairs of observations can therefore be represented by all the possible points with coordinates (x_1, x_2) within the square $OABC$ shown in fig. 2 and every point within the square is equally probable.

If $(x_2 - x_1)$ lies in $(0, Y)$ where $0 \leqslant Y \leqslant b$ then

(i) $(x_2 - x_1) \geqslant 0$ so that the point (x_1, x_2) lies above the diagonal OB, and

(ii) $(x_2 - x_1) \leqslant Y$ so that the point (x_1, x_2) lies below the line DE where OD is Y and DE is parallel to OB.

Hence if $(x_2 - x_1)$ lies in $(0, Y)$ the point (x_1, x_2) lies within the shaded area $ODEB$ and the probability of this is

$$P(0 \leqslant x_2 - x_1 \leqslant Y) = \frac{\text{shaded area } ODEB}{\text{total possible area}}$$
$$= \frac{1}{2}\left[1 - \frac{(b-Y)^2}{b^2}\right].$$

The probability that $|x_2 - x_1|$ lies in $(0, Y)$ is

$$P(0 \leqslant |x_2 - x_1| \leqslant Y) = P(0 \leqslant x_2 - x_1 \leqslant Y) + P(0 \leqslant x_1 - x_2 \leqslant Y)$$
$$= \left[1 - \frac{(b-Y)^2}{b^2}\right]$$

from which $\mathrm{d}p/\mathrm{d}Y = 2(b-Y)/b^2$ is obtained by differentiation.

Hence the frequency function of $|x_2-x_1|$ has a probability distribution

$$\mathrm{d}p = \frac{2(b-Y)}{b^2}\,\mathrm{d}Y.$$

This is the probability that $|x_2-x_1|$ lies in the interval of width $\mathrm{d}Y$ between Y and $Y+\mathrm{d}Y$. Thus the mean value of $|x_2-x_1|$ is

$$\int_0^b \frac{Y2(b-Y)}{b^2}\,\mathrm{d}Y = \tfrac{1}{3}b.$$

This implies that $|x_2-x_1|$ is an unbiased estimate of $\frac{1}{3}b$ because its mean value in sampling is $\frac{1}{3}b$ and, therefore, $3|x_2-x_1|$ is an unbiased estimate of b.

Alternatively, since the mean of (x_1+x_2) = mean of x_1+mean of x_2

$$= \tfrac{1}{2}b+\tfrac{1}{2}b$$
$$= b,$$

(x_1+x_2) is also an unbiased estimate of b.

EXAMPLE 2. *The variables x_1 and x_2 are uniformly distributed in the respective intervals (a_1, a_1+1), (a_2, a_2+1). Show how the joint probability that both x_1 and x_2 lie in specified sub-intervals can be represented by the area of a portion of a square. Hence, or otherwise, in the case $a_1 = a_2$, obtain the probability that $x_2-x_1 \leqslant X$, distinguishing the cases $-1 \leqslant X \leqslant 0$, $0 \leqslant X \leqslant 1$.*

Hence obtain a test, at the 5% level of significance, of the hypothesis $a_1 = a_2$. [Cambridge]

In fig. 3, x_1 is represented between a_1 and a_1+1 along the x-axis and x_2 between a_2 and a_2+1 along the y-axis. All the possible pairs of observations can, therefore, be represented by all the possible points with coordinates (x_1, x_2) within the square $A_1B_1C_1D_1$. Moreover, every point within the square is equally probable. As the area of the square $A_1B_1C_1D_1$ is *unity* it represents the *total joint probability* for the variables x_1 and x_2 and the area, $\delta x\cdot\delta y$, of the small shaded rectangle represents the joint probability that x_1 and x_2 lie in the specified sub-intervals δx and δy respectively.

The square $ABCD$ in fig. 4 represents the total joint probability in the case where $a_1 = a_2 = a$. In this diagram a line ODB would have the equation $y-x = 0$ and points within the square on or below DB would be such that $(x_2-x_1) \leqslant 0$. The line EF is drawn to represent

$$y-x = X \quad \text{when} \quad -1 \leqslant X \leqslant 0,$$

and the line GH is drawn to represent

$$y-x = X \quad \text{when} \quad 0 \leqslant X \leqslant 1.$$

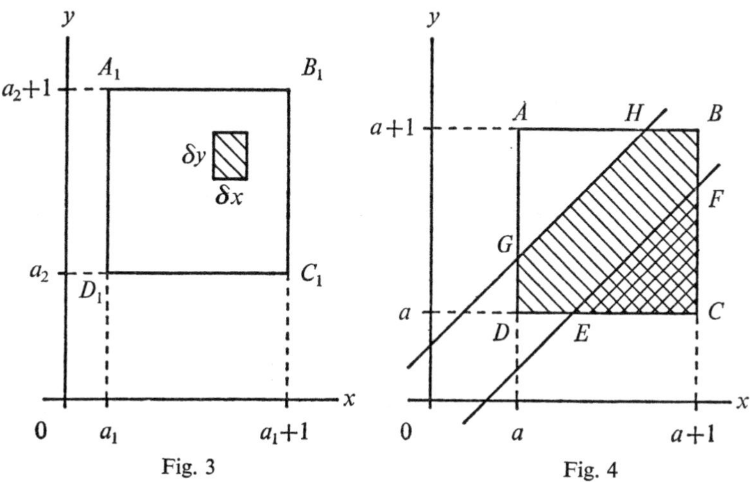

Fig. 3

Fig. 4

In case 1, the probability that $(x_2-x_1) \leqslant X$ is the shaded area

$$EFC = \tfrac{1}{2}(1+X)^2.$$

In case 2, the probability that $(x_2-x_1) \leqslant X$ is the shaded area

$$GHBCD = 1-\tfrac{1}{2}(1-X)^2.$$

To obtain a test, at the 5 % level of significance, of the hypothesis $a_1 = a_2$ the reader will find it helpful to draw the probability graph for X by plotting values as follows:

X	-1	-0.8	-0.6	-0.4	-0.2	0
Probability that $(x_2-x_1) \leqslant X$ $P\{-1 \leqslant (x_2-x_1) \leqslant X < 0\}$ $= \tfrac{1}{2}(1+X)^2$	0	0.02	0.08	0.18	0.32	0.5

X	0	0.2	0.4	0.6	0.8	1
Probability that $(x_2-x_1) \leqslant X$ $P\{0 \leqslant (x_2-x_1) \leqslant X \leqslant 1\}$ $= 1-\tfrac{1}{2}(1-X)^2$	0.5	0.68	0.82	0.92	0.98	1

From the graph and from the above table of values it can be seen that there is a 96 % probability of X lying between -0.8 and $+0.8$. To find the values of X which have a 95 % probability we have to solve

$$\tfrac{1}{2}(1+X)^2 = 0.025 \qquad (1)$$

and

$$1-\tfrac{1}{2}(1-X)^2 = 0.975. \qquad (2)$$

Equation (1) gives $X = -0.7764$ and equation (2) gives $X = 0.7764$. From this we conclude that the probability of $|x_2-x_1|$ being greater than 0.7764

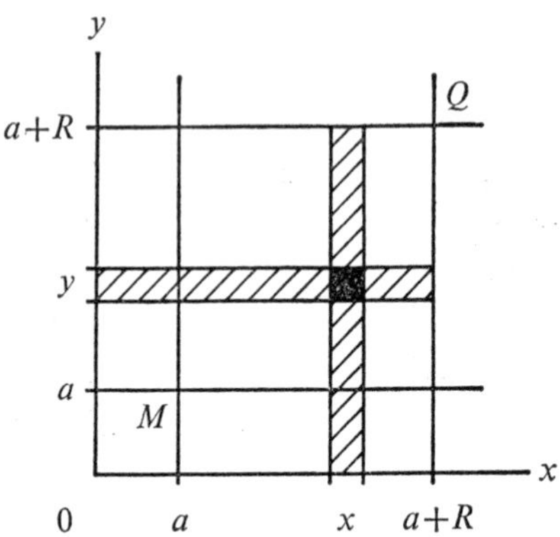

Fig. 5. The pair of observations (x_1, x_2) are uniformly distributed over the square MQ. That is to say, the probability distribution needs *three dimensions* to illustrate it diagrammatically as a *rectangular prism* of height $1/R^2$ on the square MQ as base. Its *volume* is *unity*.

is less than 5 %. This implies that, at the 5 % level of significance, the null hypothesis that $a_1 = a_2$ must be rejected if

$$|x_2-x_1| \geqslant 0.7764.$$

EXAMPLE 3. *The variable x is uniformly distributed in an interval* $(a, a+R)$, *where R is known but a is unknown. Two observations,* x_1 *and* x_2, *are made of x. Representing the joint distribution of* x_1, x_2 *on a suitable diagram, show, by considering the distribution of* x_1+x_2, *or otherwise, how to obtain an unbiased estimate of a and* 100α % *confidence limits for the estimate* (*i.e. limits* A_U *and* A_L *such that* $P(A_L \leqslant a \leqslant A_U) = \alpha$). [Cambridge]

Because x is uniformly distributed in the interval $(a, a+R)$ the probability that x_1 lies in the interval $(x-\frac{1}{2}\mathrm{d}x, x+\frac{1}{2}\mathrm{d}x)$ is $(1/R)\mathrm{d}x$ and the probability that x_2 lies in $(y-\frac{1}{2}\mathrm{d}y, y+\frac{1}{2}\mathrm{d}y)$ is $(1/R)\mathrm{d}y$. Moreover, we may assume that x_1 and x_2 are independent. Hence the probability that x_1 and x_2 respectively lie in the intervals $(x-\frac{1}{2}\mathrm{d}x, x+\frac{1}{2}\mathrm{d}x)$ and $(y-\frac{1}{2}\mathrm{d}y, y+\frac{1}{2}\mathrm{d}y)$ is $(1/R^2)\mathrm{d}x\,\mathrm{d}y$.

Thus the joint probability distribution of the (x_1, x_2) pair is

$$\int_a^{a+R}\int_a^{a+R}\frac{1}{R^2}\,\mathrm{d}x\,\mathrm{d}y = 1,$$

a rectangular prism of height $1/R^2$ on a square base of area R^2. (See fig. 5.) Hence

$$E(x_1+x_2) = \int_a^{a+R}\int_a^{a+R}(x+y)\frac{1}{R^2}\,\mathrm{d}x\,\mathrm{d}y$$
$$= 2a+R, \quad \text{by double integration.}$$

Thus (x_1+x_2) is an unbiased estimate of $2a+R$ and $\frac{1}{2}(x_1+x_2-R)$ is an unbiased estimate of a.

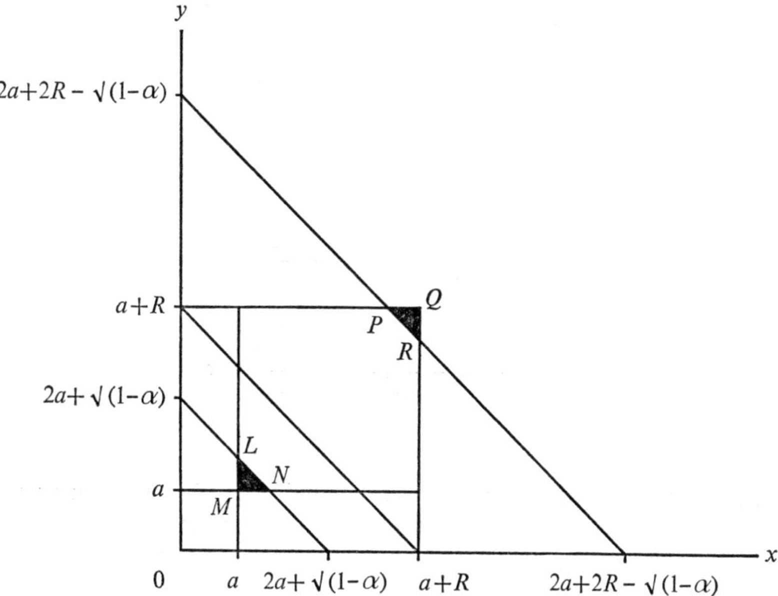

Fig. 6. The lines $x+y = 2a+\surd(1-\alpha)$ and $x+y = 2a+2R-\surd(1-\alpha)$ cut triangles LMN and PQR from the square MQ whose areas are each $\frac{1}{2}(1-\alpha)$. Thus the area of the remainder of the square is α.

Also, it can be seen from fig. 6 that the probability of $(x+y)$ lying between $2a+\surd(1-\alpha)$ and $2a+2R-\surd(1-\alpha)$ is α, i.e.

$$P\{2a+\surd(1-\alpha) < (x+y) < 2a+2R-\surd(1-\alpha)\} = \alpha.$$

Hence

$$P\{a+\tfrac{1}{2}\surd(1-\alpha)-\tfrac{1}{2}R < \tfrac{1}{2}(x+y)-\tfrac{1}{2}R < a+\tfrac{1}{2}R-\tfrac{1}{2}\surd(1-\alpha)\} = \alpha,$$

i.e.

$$P\{a-\tfrac{1}{2}[R-\surd(1-\alpha)] < \tfrac{1}{2}(x+y-R) < a+\tfrac{1}{2}[R-\surd(1-\alpha)]\} = \alpha.$$

Thus $\frac{1}{2}(x_1+x_2-R)$ is an unbiased estimate of a and its $100\alpha\,\%$ confidence limits are $\frac{1}{2}(x_1+x_2-R)\pm\frac{1}{2}[R-\surd(1-\alpha)]$.

EXAMPLE 4. *The variables x, y have joint frequency function*

$$f(x, y) = a(x-y), \quad \textit{when } x \leqslant 1,\ y \geqslant 0,\ x-y \geqslant 0,$$

and $$f(x, y) = 0, \quad \textit{elsewhere.}$$

Find the value of the constant a.

Find the frequency function of the marginal distribution of x. Show that the mean of x is $\frac{3}{4}$. *What is its median?*

Explain the meaning of the conditional distribution function $F(y|x)$. *Find, for* $x > 0$, *the value of Y satisfying the condition*

$$P(y < Y|x) = \alpha, \quad \textit{where } 0 < \alpha < 1. \qquad \text{[Cambridge]}$$

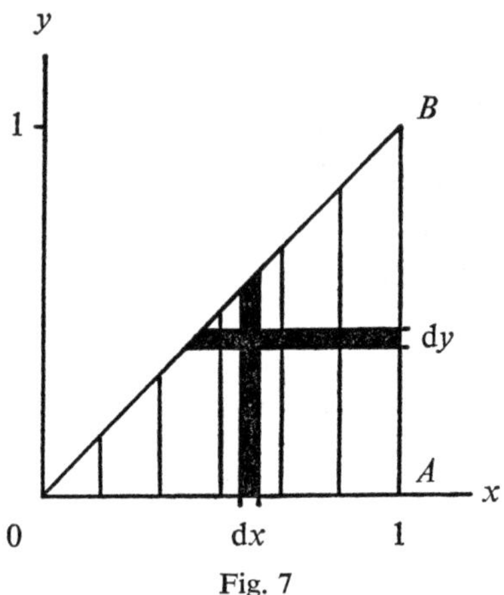

Fig. 7

The given conditions are illustrated in fig. 7. The *two-dimensional continuous* random variable (X, Y) is distributed over the triangle OAB and a must be chosen so that the double integral of $f(xy)$ over the area OAB is unity. Thus

$$\int_0^1 \int_0^x a(x-y)\,\mathrm{d}y\,\mathrm{d}x = 1, \quad \text{by summing } \mathrm{d}y \text{ first,}$$

or

$$\int_0^1 \int_y^1 a(x-y)\,\mathrm{d}x\,\mathrm{d}y = 1, \quad \text{by summing } \mathrm{d}x \text{ first.}$$

Both methods give the same result, of course, that $a = 6$. Hence the joint probability density function of (X, Y) is

$$f(x, y) = 6(x-y), \quad \text{when } x \leqslant 1,\ y \leqslant 0,\ x-y \geqslant 0,$$

and

$$f(x, y) = 0, \qquad \text{elsewhere.}$$

The *marginal probability density functions* of x and y are defined, respectively, as

$$g(x) = \int_{-\infty}^{\infty} f(x, y)\,\mathrm{d}y \quad \text{and} \quad h(y) = \int_{-\infty}^{\infty} f(x, y)\,\mathrm{d}x.$$

Thus, in the case under consideration, the frequency function of the marginal distribution of x is

$$g(x) = \int_0^x 6(x-y)\,\mathrm{d}y,$$

by integrating over the vertical strip of fig. 7. Thus

$$g(x) = 3x^2.$$

TABLE 6A. *Two-dimensional probability distribution of the given random variable* (X, Y)

Y	X: 0–$\frac{1}{6}$	$\frac{1}{6}$–$\frac{1}{3}$	$\frac{1}{3}$–$\frac{1}{2}$	$\frac{1}{2}$–$\frac{2}{3}$	$\frac{2}{3}$–$\frac{5}{6}$	$\frac{5}{6}$–1	Marginal probability distribution of Y
0–$\frac{1}{6}$	1/216	6/216	12/216	18/216	24/216	30/216	91/216
$\frac{1}{6}$–$\frac{1}{3}$	0	1/216	6/216	12/216	18/216	24/216	61/216
$\frac{1}{3}$–$\frac{1}{2}$	0	0	1/216	6/216	12/216	18/216	37/216
$\frac{1}{2}$–$\frac{2}{3}$	0	0	0	1/216	6/216	12/216	19/216
$\frac{2}{3}$–$\frac{5}{6}$	0	0	0	0	1/216	6/216	7/216
$\frac{5}{6}$–1	0	0	0	0	0	1/216	1/216
Marginal probability distribution of X	1/216	7/216	19/216	37/216	61/216	91/216	1

This implies that the probabilities

$$P(0 \leqslant X \leqslant \tfrac{1}{6}),\, P(\tfrac{1}{6} \leqslant X \leqslant \tfrac{1}{3}),\, \ldots,\, P(\tfrac{5}{6} \leqslant X \leqslant 1)$$

are given, respectively, by

$$\int_0^{\frac{1}{6}} g(x)\,\mathrm{d}x = 1/216, \int_{\frac{1}{6}}^{\frac{1}{3}} g(x)\,\mathrm{d}x = 7/216, \ldots, \int_{\frac{5}{6}}^{1} g(x)\,\mathrm{d}x = 91/216.$$

These values are shown as the marginal probability distribution of X in table 6A and illustrated geometrically by the six slices of the tretrahedron in fig. 8.

Also, the frequency function of the marginal distribution of Y is

$$h(y) = \int_y^1 6(x-y)\,\mathrm{d}x,$$

by integrating over the horizontal strip of fig. 7. Thus

$$h(y) = 3(1-y)^2.$$

Thus the marginal probability distribution of Y stated in table 6A is

$$P(0 \leqslant Y \leqslant \tfrac{1}{6}),\, P(\tfrac{1}{6} \leqslant Y \leqslant \tfrac{1}{3}),\, \ldots,\, P(\tfrac{5}{6} \leqslant Y \leqslant 1)$$

given, respectively, by

$$\int_0^{\frac{1}{6}} h(y)\,\mathrm{d}y = 91/216, \int_{\frac{1}{6}}^{\frac{1}{3}} h(y)\,\mathrm{d}y = 61/216, \ldots, \int_{\frac{5}{6}}^{1} h(y)\,\mathrm{d}y = 1/216.$$

The reader will find it an interesting exercise to check the other probabilities in table 6A.

The mean of X,

$$\begin{aligned} E(X) &= \int_0^1 \int_0^x x f(x, y)\,\mathrm{d}y\,\mathrm{d}x \\ &= \int_0^1 \int_0^x 6(x^2 - xy)\,\mathrm{d}y\,\mathrm{d}x \\ &= \tfrac{3}{4}. \end{aligned}$$

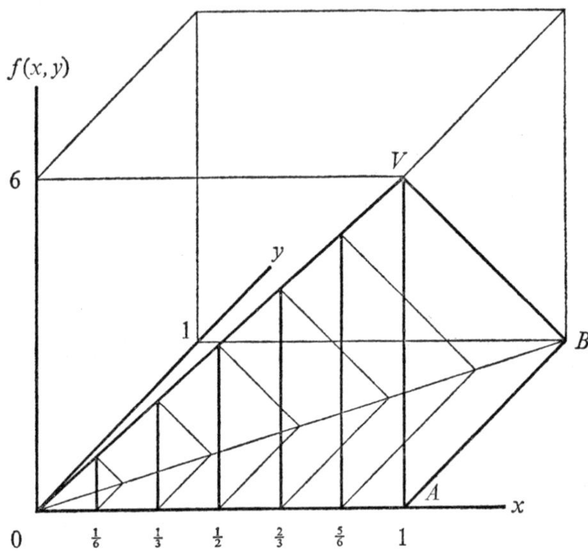

Fig. 8. The tetrahedron $OABV$ has unit volume. The base OAB is the right-angled triangle shown in fig. 7. The perpendicular height AV (not to scale) is 6 units. The six slices of the tetrahedron have volumes

$$1/216, \quad 7/216, \quad 19/216, \quad 37/216, \quad 61/216, \quad 91/216$$

which represent the marginal probability distribution of x.

This agrees with a well-known property of solid tetrahedra. The median of X, the 50th percentile p_{50}, is given by

$$\int_0^{p_{50}} \int_0^{x} f(x, y)\, \mathrm{d}y\, \mathrm{d}x = \tfrac{1}{2},$$

from which we find $p_{50} = 2^{-\frac{1}{3}} = 0.79$ (2 decimals). This indicates that the plane $x = 0.79$ divides the volume of the tetrahedron $OABV$ into two equal parts. This fact could be deduced, for the tetrahedron, by pure geometry of course but not for the general joint frequency function, $f(x, y)$.

The conditional distribution function of Y for a given value of $X = x$ is defined by

$$F(y|x) = \frac{f(x, y)}{g(x)}, \quad g(x) > 0.$$

Thus, in the case under consideration,

$$F(y|x) = \frac{6(x-y)}{3x^2}, \\ = \frac{2(x-y)}{x^2}.$$

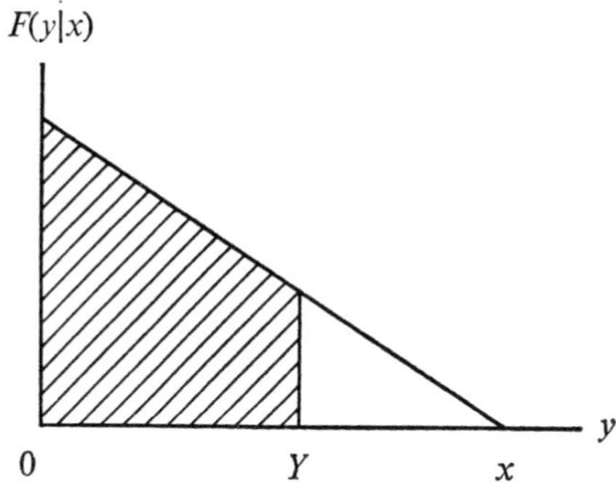

Fig. 9. The shaded area illustrates $P(y < Y|x)$.

Suppose the tetrahedron $OABV$ of fig. 8 is sliced by a plane $x = C$ the resulting right-angled triangle is the one-dimensional distribution called the distribution of Y for $X = C$. Hence, the sections shown in the diagram are

$$F(y|\tfrac{1}{6}),\ F(y|\tfrac{1}{3}),\ \ldots,\ F(y|1).$$

Note that the conditional distribution satisfies the requirements

$$F(y|x) \geqslant 0$$

and
$$\int_{-\infty}^{\infty} F(y|x)\,\mathrm{d}y = \int_0^x \frac{2(x-y)}{x^2}\,\mathrm{d}y$$
$$= \frac{2}{x^2}\,[xy-\tfrac{1}{2}y^2]_0^x$$
$$= 1.$$

For a given value of $X = x$, the probability of y being less than Y

$$P(y < Y|x) = \int_0^Y \frac{2(x-y)}{x^2}\,\mathrm{d}y$$
$$= \frac{2}{x^2}\,(xY-\tfrac{1}{2}Y^2).$$

This is illustrated by the shaded area of fig. 9 and if

$$\frac{2}{x^2}\,(xY-\tfrac{1}{2}Y^2) = \alpha, \quad \text{where } 0 < \alpha < 1,$$

then
$$Y^2-2xY+x^2\alpha = 0.$$

Hence
$$Y = x \pm x\sqrt{(1-\alpha)}.$$

However, since Y must lie between 0 and x, the + sign is impossible and we may finally write

$$Y = x-x\sqrt{(1-\alpha)}.$$

7

MISCELLANEOUS EXERCISES

1. Assuming that the (cumulative) distribution function $\Phi(x)$ is known, when $x \geqslant 0$, for the standard Normal distribution with mean 0 and variance 1, obtain an expression for the probability that a Normal variable X, with mean μ and variance σ^2, takes a value between a and b, where $a < \mu < b$.

The average number of hours per week which male students at a particular university spend in study is known to be 25 hours with a standard deviation of 6 hours. The corresponding figures for female students are 28 hours and 5 hours respectively. Calculate the probability that, in a given week, the average week's work of a random sample of 5 men and 2 women students will lie between 24 and 31. Calculate also the probability that the average week's work of two women will differ by more than 8 hours. (N.B. For both male and female students the number of hours worked should be assumed to have a Normal distribution.) [Cambridge]

Hint. The *total* must lie between 168 and 217 hours.

2. Through a fixed point P on a circle of unit radius a random chord is drawn, such that the angle between the chord and the diameter through P is uniformly distributed in $(-\frac{1}{2}\pi, \frac{1}{2}\pi)$. Show that the distribution of the length of the larger of the two parts into which the circumference is divided is uniform in $(\pi, 2\pi)$.

Find also the mean value of the area of the larger of the two parts of the circle, and the mean length of the chord. [Northern]

3. Define the Poisson distribution and calculate its mean. State how it may be approximated under suitable conditions by a Normal distribution.

In a community with a large number of drivers an average of 100 are involved in accidents each year. In a certain year 120 have accidents: carry out a significance test to discover whether this represents a real increase. [Northern]

4. In the equation $$x^2+2x-a = 0$$

a has a rectangular distribution on the interval (0, 2). Find the distribution of the larger root.

Find the probability that, of six equations

$$x^2+2x-a = 0$$

in each of which a is taken independently from the rectangular distribution on (0, 2), no more than one has its larger root greater than $\sqrt{2}-1$. [Northern]

5. (i) Define the Binomial distribution, and explain why it might be expected to be appropriate in the treatment of the problem in (ii).

(ii) A product is made up into batches of 5 for distribution, and in 90 such batches there is a total of 135 faulty items.

Obtain a confidence interval for p, the probability that a single item will be faulty. Deduce a confidence interval for the average number of faulty items in a batch. (You may use the Normal approximation.) [Northern]

6. Let $x_1, x_2, ..., x_n$ be n observations from a distribution with mean μ and variance σ^2, and let $\bar{x}$ be the sample mean. Write down the expectation and the variance of $\bar{x}$.

It is known that $\mu = \sigma$, and it is desired to estimate μ by an estimator of the form $k\bar{x}$, where k is to be chosen in such a way as to minimise the expectation of $(k\bar{x}-\mu)^2$. Find the value of k. [Northern]

7. Let $\bar{x}$ be the mean of n observations, $x_1, x_2, ..., x_n$ drawn from a Normal distribution with unknown mean μ and known variance $\sigma^2 = 1$. Explain how a test of significance of the null hypothesis $\mu = 0$ against two-sided alternatives may be carried out. Show that the test will reject the null hypothesis, if and only if zero lies outside a certain confidence interval for μ.

(*a*) Determine (i) the smallest value of n, for which $\bar{x} = 0.15$ would result in rejection of the hypothesis $\mu = 0$ at the 5 % significance level, (ii) the 95 % confidence interval for μ for these values of n and $\bar{x}$.

(*b*) If $\mu = 1$ and $n = 10$, find the probability that the wrong conclusion is drawn from a test of the above type constructed at the 5 % level for the hypothesis $\mu = 0$. [Northern]

Hint. See Glossary for (*a*) Interval estimate and (*b*) Type I and Type II errors.

8. The lengths of mass-produced components are Normally distributed about the value 150 mm with standard deviation 0.3 mm and each costs 8p to produce. A component shorter than 149.5 mm has to be scrapped, whereas a component longer than 150.5 mm can be trimmed at a further cost of 3p. Components having lengths between these limits are satisfactory and cost the manufacturer nothing extra.

(*a*) Calculate the expected cost of producing an acceptable component.

(*b*) What is the probability that out of 100 randomly selected components before inspection at least 90 are satisfactory? [Institute of Statisticians]

9. The probability distribution defined by the distribution function

$$F(x) = 1 - \exp(-\lambda x)$$

for $x \geqslant 0$ where $\lambda > 0$, is known as a negative exponential distribution with parameter λ. Find the corresponding density function of x, and show that the mean and the standard deviation are equal.

Show that for a Poisson process with an average λ failures per unit time, the time interval from one failure to the next has a negative exponential distribution. [Institute of Statisticians]

10. A rolling machine in a paper mill produces on average one flaw every 150 m of paper. Assuming that the number of flaws in a given length of paper has a Poisson distribution, find the probability that

(*a*) a 600 m roll has no flaws,

(*b*) a 150 m roll has at most three flaws,

(*c*) out of three 300 m rolls, one has one flaw and the others have none.
[Institute of Statisticians]

11. Packets of detergents sell at the same price.

Ten packets of Ono were bought, but only seven packets of Draff could be obtained. The weights of detergent in the packets of the two types were found to be, in grams:

Ono: 860, 871, 852, 891, 817, 883, 848, 865, 871, 859
Draff: 886, 891, 885, 890, 893, 899, 871.

Is there any reason to suppose that

(i) the weight in packets of Draff is more consistent than in packets of Ono,

(ii) the average weight in packets of Draff is greater than the average weight in packets of Ono? [A.E.B.]

Hint. See Glossary for (i) *F*-test (ii) Significance of difference between means.

12. A process for making electric light bulbs produces, on the average, one bulb in 100 defective, when under control. Use the Poisson distribution to calculate the probability that a sample of 50 will contain (i) 0 (ii) 1 or (iii) 2 defective bulbs.

The bulbs are delivered in batches of 1000, from which 50 are taken at random. If at most one of the 50 is found to be defective, the whole batch is accepted. Calculate the probability of accepting a batch containing 50 defective bulbs. [A.E.B.]

13. The variable z is Normal with mean μ and known variance σ^4; the mean of n independent observations of z is $\bar{z}$. The Normal table gives the integral

$$\Phi(x) = \frac{1}{\sqrt{(2\pi)}}\int_{-\infty}^{x} e^{-\frac{1}{2}t^2}\,dt.$$

Explain how this table may be used to find an interval (Z_1, Z_2) such that if $\bar{z}$ falls outside the interval we reject at the α % level of significance the null hypothesis $\mu = \mu_0$.

Explain further how to calculate the probability of rejecting this null hypothesis when in fact $\mu = \mu_1 > \mu_0$. Obtain this probability for $\mu_1 = 1.8$, given that $n = 16$, $\sigma = 2.041$, $\alpha = 5$, $\mu_0 = 1.0$. [Cambridge]

14. The variable x has variance σ^2, which is estimated from independent observations $x_1, x_2, \ldots, x_n$ by

$$s^2 = \frac{1}{n-1}\sum_{i=1}^{n}(x_i-\bar{x})^2, \quad \text{where} \quad \bar{x} = \frac{1}{n}\sum_{i=1}^{n}x_i.$$

Prove that s^2 is an unbiased estimate of σ^2; you may assume $\text{var}(\bar{x}) = \sigma^2 n$.

Compare the arithmetical advantages of the forms

$$\sum_{i=1}^{n} (x_i - \bar{x})^2 \quad \text{and} \quad \sum_{i=1}^{n} x_i^2 - \frac{1}{n}\left(\sum_{i=1}^{n} x_i\right)^2$$

in calculation. Obtain the relationship between

$$\sum_{i=1}^{n} (x_i - \bar{x})^2 \quad \text{and} \quad \sum_{i=1}^{n} (y_i - \bar{y})^2,$$

where $y_i = b(x_i - a)$ for constant a and b, and explain how this relationship may be used to simplify the calculation of s^2.

Estimate σ^2 from the observations

93.17, 92.94, 92.81, 93.04, 93.08, 93.05. [Cambridge]

15. All the n rats in a group are given a standard dose of a poison. Before each rat is dosed we can say with certainty that it will either die or not die; what then is the meaning of the statement 'the probability that a rat will die when dosed is p'?

Show that the probability that r deaths result from the experiment is

$$\binom{n}{r} p^r(1-p)^{n-r} \quad (0 \leqslant r \leqslant n).$$

Show also that the expectation of r is np, and state its variance.

Illustrate the use of the Normal distribution as an approximation to the Binomial distribution by using it to calculate the probability of more than 60 deaths when $n = 100$ and $p = \frac{1}{2}$. [Cambridge]

16. Describe in what sense the process of calculating expectation for a population is related to that of calculating average in a sample.

The variable x is uniformly distributed in (0, 2). Obtain, to 3 significant figures, the mean and variance of x and of $\sin x$. Obtain to the same accuracy approximate values for the mean and variance of $\sin x$ by using the formulae:

$$E[f(x)] \doteqdot f(\mu) + \tfrac{1}{2}\sigma^2 f''(\mu),$$

$$\text{var}\,[f(x)] \doteqdot \sigma^2[f'(\mu)]^2,$$

where $\mu = E(x)$, $\sigma^2 = \text{var}\,(x)$. [Cambridge]

17. The currency of a certain country consists of notes for 5, 10, 100 and 1000 cents; the percentages *by value* of the total currency formed by these notes are 1.6 %, 2.4 %, 16 % and 80 %. Two issues of notes are in circulation: the proportions of old to new issue in the four denominations are 3:2, 1:1, 2:3 and 1:4. Calculate

(*a*) the value of the old issue of notes as a percentage of the total currency,

(*b*) the percentages *by number* of the four denominations in the total currency,

(*c*) the percentage *by number* of old notes which are of the 5 cent denomination,

(*d*) the ratio of the mean values of the old and new issues. [Cambridge]

18. State precisely the conditions under which a variable may be expected to have a Binomial distribution. Give *two* examples where these conditions are satisfied.

A fly moves on a line. Starting from the origin it moves at each second either unit distance in the positive direction or, with equal probability, unit distance in the negative direction. Obtain and plot the distributions of the fly's position after (*a*) 4 and (*b*) 5 seconds.

Obtain the mean and variance of its distance from the origin after t seconds.

When the fly reaches a distance 6 or more units from the origin in the positive direction it is trapped. Show that the probability that it is trapped within 8 seconds is 5/128. [Cambridge]

19. In a certain village the number of single births of children in a week is a Poisson variable with mean n_1, and the number of twin births in a week is an independent Poisson variable with mean n_2.

Determine the mean and variance of the number, N, of children born in a week.

Say whether you consider that the distribution of N is of the Poisson form, and justify your answer.

What is the probability that five children are born in any given week? [Cambridge]

20. The average speeds of a number of vehicles each making the same journey of 40 miles may be assumed to be rectangularly distributed over the interval 20 m.p.h. to 40 m.p.h. Find the probability distribution of the time T taken to make the journey. For what proportion of vehicles will T lie between 1 h 30 min and 1 h 45 min? [Northern]

21. The points P and Q are randomly and independently located on a circle of radius a. Obtain and plot the distribution function of the length (regarded as positive) of the minor arc PQ. Find the mean and variance of this length.

Obtain and plot the frequency and distribution functions of the length of the chord PQ. [Cambridge]

22. A certain gravel may be assumed to consist entirely of spherical stones whose diameters follow a Normal distribution with mean 2 cm and standard deviation 0.5 cm. Five wire sieves are used in succession to divide the gravel into six grades. The diameters of the first and fifth sieves are chosen so that 5 % of the stones (by number) are retained by the first sieve and 5 % are passed by the fifth. The other three sieves are chosen so that the remaining four fractions contain equal numbers of stones. Find to the nearest tenth of a millimetre the diameters of the holes in the five sieves.

Determine the percentages (by number) of stones in the six grades if the mean diameter of the gravel increases to 2.5 cm, the standard deviation remaining unchanged. [Cambridge]

23. The variable x is uniformly distributed in (0, 2). Obtain and plot the frequency and distribution functions of x.

Two independent observations, x_1 and x_2, are made of x. Show how to represent their joint distribution on a square in a suitable diagram. Hence or otherwise obtain and plot the frequency and distribution functions of $X = x_1+x_2$. [Cambridge]

Hint. $x_1+x_2 = X$ is the straight line which makes equal intercepts, X, on the axes of x_1 and x_2. If dA is the area cut from the above square by the lines

$$x_1+x_2 = X \quad \text{and} \quad x_1+x_2 = X+dX$$

then
$$f(X)\,dX = \tfrac{1}{4}dA$$

because (x_1, x_2) is uniformly distributed over the square with probability $\frac{1}{4}$.

24. The random variable X is uniformly distributed in the range $-a \leqslant x \leqslant 3a$. The random variable Z is related to X by

$$\begin{aligned} Z &= 0, && \text{if } X \leqslant 0,\\ Z &= X/a, && \text{if } 0 \leqslant X \leqslant a,\\ Z &= 1, && \text{if } X \geqslant a. \end{aligned}$$

Calculate the (cumulative) distribution function, the mean and the variance of Z. Give a sketch of the distribution function of Z. [Cambridge]

25. The variables r and θ have joint frequency function $f(r, \theta)$. Define

(*a*) the expectation of any function $g(r, \theta)$,

(*b*) the variance of r,

(*c*) the covariance of r and θ.

The point (r, θ) lies in the first quadrant of a circle of radius a; r is uniformly distributed in $(0, a)$ and θ is independently uniformly distributed in $(0, \frac{1}{2}\pi)$. Find the mean and variance of $x\,(= r\cos\theta)$, and the covariance of x and $y\,(= r\sin\theta)$. [Cambridge]

26. The variables x_1, x_2 have means $\alpha\theta$, $\beta\theta$, variances σ_1^2, σ_2^2 and covariance C. Give formulae for the mean and variance of $X = \lambda x_1+\mu x_2$, where λ, μ are constants.

Show how to choose λ, μ so that $E(X) = \theta$.

Subject to this condition determine, in the special case $C = 0$, the values of λ, μ which minimise the variance of X. Show that if $\alpha = \beta = 1$ these values are

$$\lambda = \frac{\sigma_2^2}{\sigma_1^2+\sigma_2^2}, \quad \mu = \frac{\sigma_1^2}{\sigma_1^2+\sigma_2^2}.$$

[Cambridge]

27. For the $n(x, y)$ pairs $(x_1, y_1), (x_2, y_2), \ldots, (x_n, y_n)$ with mean $(\bar{x}, \bar{y})$, the sums of squares and products are calculated from the formulae

$$S_{xx} = \sum_{i=1}^{n} (x_i-\bar{x})^2,$$

$$S_{yy} = \sum_{i=1}^{n} (y_i-\bar{y})^2,$$

$$S_{xy} = \sum_{i=1}^{n} (x_i-\bar{x})(y_i-\bar{y}).$$

The constants a and b in the regression equation

$$y = a+b(x-\bar{x})$$

are obtained by minimising the value of R given by

$$R = \sum_{i=1}^{n} [y_i - a - b(x_i-\bar{x})]^2.$$

Show that R can be expressed as

$$R = (S_{yy}-S_{xy}{}^2/S_{xx})+n(a-\bar{y})^2+(bS_{xx}-S_{xy})^2/S_{xx},$$

and hence deduce that the minimum value of R is

$$S_{yy}-S_{xy}{}^2/S_{xx},$$

when $a = \bar{y}$ and $b = S_{xy}/S_{xx}$.

28. The variables x, y are observed together n times, giving values x_1, y_1; x_2, y_2; ...; x_n, y_n. The sums of squares and products are calculated from the formulae

$$S_{xx} = \sum_{i=1}^{n} (x_i-\bar{x})^2,$$

$$S_{xy} = \sum_{i=1}^{n} (x_i-\bar{x})(y_i-\bar{y}),$$

$$S_{yy} = \sum_{i=1}^{n} (y_i-\bar{y})^2.$$

The average relationship between x and y may be assumed to be a straight line of unknown gradient β through the point $(\bar{x}, \bar{y})$, so that the value, Y_i, predicted for any given x_i is

$$Y_i = \bar{y}+\beta(x_i-\bar{x}).$$

Show that the value of β which minimises the expression

$$R = \sum_{i=1}^{n} (y_i - Y_i)^2$$

is S_{xy}/S_{xx}, and find the minimum value of R.

The following values were obtained from 12 pairs of observations:

$$\bar{x} = 4, \quad \bar{y} = 5; \quad S_{xx} = 10, \quad S_{xy} = -15, \quad S_{yy} = 25.$$

Plot the line which minimises R. [Cambridge]

29. The following table gives the value observed for the dependent variable y which is subject to experimental error, when an independent variable is adjusted to have the value x.

x	0	1	2	3	4
y	0.51	0.99	1.61	2.02	2.48

Plot the values of y against x and ascertain which one of them appears to be grossly in error.

Using the remaining four values only, find the equation of the regression line of y on x. What value does the regression equation predict for the aberrant observation?

Assuming that each y value is the mean of 36 independent determinations each with the same standard deviation 0.22, and that the predicted value is effectively the true mean value of the variable y, find the probability of such a mean of observations being as aberrant as or more aberrant than the one in question. [Cambridge]

30. The variables x and y are observed together n times, giving values x_1, y_1; x_2, y_2; ...; x_n, y_n, with means $\bar{x}, \bar{y}$. Explain how an estimate, r, of the correlation coefficient can be calculated from these values. What is the geometrical meaning of the sign of r?

By considering the minimum with respect to variations of λ of

$$G(\lambda) = \sum_{i=1}^{n} [y_i - \bar{y} - \lambda(x_i - \bar{x})]^2,$$

or otherwise, show that $|r| \leqslant 1$.

Illustrate, for example by a scatter diagram, a case where there is a close relationship between x and y and yet r is near to zero. [Cambridge]

ANSWERS TO EXERCISES

Preliminary revision exercises

1. (i) 30–33, 47–50, 75–78; 95. (ii) 49, 20; $y = \frac{1}{2}x + 30\frac{1}{2}$.

2. (*a*) (i) 302400; (ii) 48; (iii) $\frac{11}{60}$. (*b*) $\frac{9}{23}$.

3. (i) -0.95; (ii) $y = -0.107x + 29.7$; (iii) 24.

4. (*a*) (i) 0.0344; (ii) 0.0168; (iii) 0.1056; (iv) 0.0455. (*b*) Sig.

5. (*b*) Not sufficient.

6. (i) 50; 41, 62. (ii) 50.7, 17.0; 50.7, 39.2, 62.2.

7. (*a*) 241/969; (*b*) Not sufficient; (*c*) 6.

8. 25983, 35704, 24924. (i) 0.82. (ii) $y = -1.414 + 0.959x$; 46.5.

9. (ii) 0.6014.

10. (i) 0.026, 0.130, 0.197. (ii) 0.027, 0.121, 0.199.

12. (*a*) 489600; (*b*) 14280; (*c*) 1/1140, 13/95, 34/95.

13. 4.045, -0.04633; 57.1, 0.04633; 7.1.

14. (*a*) 0.0463, 0.00168; (*b*) Sufficient.

15. (*b*) 0.2119.

16. 1.35; 0.19; 0.21.

17. (*a*) 158; (*b*) 1/136, 15/68, 105/136.

18. (i) 48 kg; (ii) $x = 8y + 1216$; (iii) 0.8.

21. 1.56, 1.56, 1.73, 1.73, 1.73, 1.8, 1.8;
1.56, 1.56, 1.42, 1.42, 1.42, 1.42, 1.42, 1.56.

22. 14/55, 28/55, 12/55, 1/55.

23. 0.296, 0.381, 0.323; 10, 2.887, 6 % (continuity).

24. $y = 3.12x - 15.8$, 0.937; 16-year-old.

25. Yes.

§**6.** **1.** (iv) 0.675, -0.675.

2. (i) $(x-a)/(b-a)$; (ii) $\frac{1}{2}(b+a)$, $\frac{1}{12}(b-a)^2$.

3. (i) $(1 - e^{-\lambda x})$; (ii) $1/\lambda$, $\ln 2/\lambda$, 0, $1/\lambda^2$.

4. 22/15; 11/225; 0.0784. **5.** 3/32; 4, 0.8.

6. 3; 3. **7.** $n+1$; $n+1$. **8.** $13e^{-3} = 0.6474$.

9. $\frac{1}{2}x^2$ if $0 \leqslant x \leqslant 1$; $-1+2x-\frac{1}{2}x^2$ if $1 \leqslant x \leqslant 2$; 1 if $2 \leqslant x \leqslant 3$.

11. $1-6e^{-5}+15e^{-4}-10e^{-3}$. **12.** 602000 litres.

13. $b = 0$, $a \geqslant 1$, $3/2(3a-1)$; $a = 1$. **14.** $n!$

15. 4; 1; $6e^{-2}(1-3e^{-2})$.

16. 1, 2; $27e^{-4}(1-2e^{-2}) = 0.36$; 0.40.

17. $-\frac{2}{3}$. (*a*) 0.337; (*b*) $\frac{3}{8}$.

18. $\mu_2 = \frac{1}{2}$, $\mu_3 = \frac{1}{5}$, skewed positively, $\mu_4 = \frac{3}{5}$, platykurtic.

§26. **1.** 7.8p. **2.** 1.79 m; 0.071 m; 2.0 m.

3. 0.24. **4.** 2.275 %.

5. $100\{\Phi(x_2)-\Phi(x_1)\}$ per cent
where $x_2 = (b-\mu)/\sigma$ and $x_1 = (a-\mu)/\sigma$, $b > a$,
using $\Phi(-x) = 1-\Phi(x)$ for $x < 0$.
(*a*) 0.480; (*b*) 0.432; (*c*) 0.488.

6. 7.87 %; 7.87 %. **7.** 0.3974.

8. 13.5; 24.75. **9.** ± 0.877 ohms.

10. 0.0125 mm.

11. 0.4 %; mean $(x+y) = 16$ p.p.2m; var$(x+y) = 4.5$ (p.p.2m)^2; 0.01 %; 7.6×10^{-7} %.

12. 4.3 %; mean $(x+y) = 92$ p.p.2m; var$(x+y) = 98$ (p.p.2m)^2; 0.8 %.

§32. **2.** (i) 0.000518; (ii) 0.000503, 5.651 ± 0.0014.

3. 1.42 ± 0.99. **4.** 1.71, 2.43.

§41. **1.** 0.02. **2.** 0.1348; 2.5, 1.5. **3.** 0.1016; 0.0774.

4. (i) 0.0007, 0.006, 0.026, 0.069, 0.129, 0.181, 0.196, 0.168, 0.116, 0.064, 0.029, 0.011, 0.003.
(ii) 0.002, 0.009, 0.027, 0.065, 0.121, 0.176, 0.199, 0.176, 0.121, 0.065, 0.027, 0.009, 0.002.

5. 0.014, 0.054, 0.114, 0.140. (ii) 0.015, 0.051, 0.110, 0.141.

6. 0.002, 0.028, 0.122, 0.196, 0.122, 0.028, 0.002.
(ii) 0.002, 0.027, 0.121, 0.199, 0.121, 0.027, 0.002.

7. (i) 0.004, 0.024, 0.071, 0.136, 0.187, 0.196, 0.163, 0.111, 0.062, 0.029, 0.012.
(ii) 0.009, 0.027, 0.065, 0.121, 0.176, 0.199, 0.176, 0.121, 0.065, 0.027, 0.009.

8. (i) Improvement significant at 5 % level; (ii) compatible.

9. No; 40 to 60 %. **10.** 52; no.

11. p, $p(1-p)$; np, $np(1-p)$. **12.** 0.2; no.

14. (*a*) $(1-p_4)^6\,(1+6p_4+21p_4^2)$.
(*b*) (i) $p_1p_{1a}+p_2p_{2a}+p_3p_{3a}$; (ii) $p_4+p_1p_{1c}+p_2p_{2c}+p_3p_{3c}$.
(*c*) $(1-p_1p_{1a}-p_2p_{2a}-p_3p_{3a})^4$.

§51. **1.** $m = 0.63$; 53, 34, 11, 2, 0; $\nu = 1$, $\chi^2 = 0.71$; not sig.

2. $m = 0.5$; 65.5, 32.8, 9.7; $\nu = 1$, $\chi^2 = 3.77$; evidence that suicides do *not* occur independently is *not* significant.

3. $m = 1.217$; 105, 128, 78, $31\frac{1}{2}$, $9\frac{1}{2}$, $2\frac{1}{2}$, $\frac{1}{2}$; $\nu = 3$, $\chi^2 = 3.58$; not sig.

4. 0.8. **5.** 0.1845; 0.4.

6. (i) 1; (ii) 0.846; (iii) 0.013. **7.** $\binom{10}{4} p^4q^6 = 0.22.$

8. (*a*) 0.00674; (*b*) 0.0103, 0.17.

9. (i) 3.48, 2.77. (ii) 6.9, 9.3, 10.8, 9.4, 6.6, 7.0; $\nu = 4$; $\chi^2 = 3.39$. (iii) $e^{-13.92} = 10^{-6}$ approx.

11. 1.5, 1.6; $\nu = 3$; $\chi^2 = 5.32$; 0.78.

12. $m = 3.863$; 6.3, 24.4, 47.1, 60.6, 58.6, 45.3, 29.2, 16.1, 12.4; $\nu = 7$; $\chi^2 = 31.3$; 0.1 % level; not random.

13. (i) $\sigma^2 = 1.83$. (ii) 18, 34, 32, 21, 10, 5; $\nu = 4$; $\chi^2 = 1.53$. (iii) 1.79.

14. (*a*) 0.00674. (*b*) 0.1247; $P(x \geqslant 3) = 0.08$ indicates 'yes'.

15. $e^{-nm} m^{n\bar{r}}/(1!\,2!\,3!\,\ldots)(f_0 f_1 f_2 \ldots)$
where $\bar{r} = \{\Sigma i f_i\}/n$, $\hat{m} = \bar{r}$, $\text{var}(\hat{m}) = m/n$.

§53. **1.** $2\frac{1}{3}$, $\frac{34}{45}$. **2.** $468\frac{3}{4}$, 63756.

3. $7\pi/3$, $34\pi^2/45$. **4.** $3(2-\sqrt{3})/(2\pi)$, 0.005.

§57. **1.** Trials independent; each has 2 outcomes; p is constant, $a_1 = a_2 = 1/(r_1+r_2)$.

2. $a_1 = a_2 = \frac{1}{2}$; $\text{var}(X) = \frac{1}{2}\text{var}(x)$; $\text{var}(X) = 1/n(\text{var}\,x)$; 5; 0.67.

Miscellaneous exercises

1. $\Phi\{(b-\mu)/\sigma\} + \Phi\{(\mu-a)/\sigma\} - 1$; 0.7955, 0.258.

2. $(3\pi^2+4)/4\pi$; $4/\pi$. **3.** $1-\Phi(19\frac{1}{2}/10) = 2\frac{1}{2}$ % level.

4. $f(y) = y+1$, $0 \leqslant y \leqslant \sqrt{3}-1$; $\frac{7}{64}$.

5. (ii) 95 % C.I. are $\dfrac{135}{450} \pm \dfrac{1.96}{450}\left[135\left(1-\dfrac{135}{450}\right)\right]^{\frac{1}{2}} = 0.3 \pm 0.04$; 1.5 ± 0.2.

6. $n/(n+1)$.

7. $P(-1.96/\sqrt{n} < \bar{x} < 1.96/\sqrt{n}) = 0.95$;
$P(\bar{x}-1.96/\sqrt{n} < 0 < \bar{x}+1.96/\sqrt{n}) = 0.95$.
(*a*) (i) 171; (ii) $0 < \mu < 0.30$. (*b*) $\Phi(1.62)+\Phi(0.38)-1 = 0.5954$.

8. (*a*) $8.55p$; (*b*) 0.63 (continuity). **10.** (*a*) 0.018; (*b*) 0.98; (*c*) 0.015.

11. (i) $F = 5.48$, not quite sig. at 5 % level; (ii) $t = 3.16$, sig. at 1 % level.

12. (i) 0.6065; (ii) 0.3033; (iii) 0.0758, 0.287.

13. 0.3478. **14.** 0.01555. **15.** 0.02275.

16. 1, 0.333; 0.708, 0.0932; 0.701, 0.0973.

17. (*a*) 24.56; (*b*) 40, 30, 20, 10; (*c*) 24; (*d*) 0.339.

18. (*a*) distances -4, -2, 0, 2, 4, with probabilities $\frac{1}{16}$, $\frac{1}{4}$, $\frac{3}{8}$, $\frac{1}{4}$, $\frac{1}{16}$.
(*b*) distances -5, -3, -1, 1, 3, 5, with probabilities $\frac{1}{32}$, $\frac{5}{32}$, $\frac{5}{16}$, $\frac{5}{16}$, $\frac{5}{32}$, $\frac{1}{32}$,
0, $\frac{1}{2}t$.

19. n_1+2n_2, n_1+2n_2; $e^{-(n_1+2n_2)}(n_1+2n_2)^5/5!$.

20. $f(t) = 2t^{-2}$, $1 \leqslant t \leqslant 2$; $F(t) = 2-2/t$; $\frac{4}{21}$.

21. $F(x) = x/\pi a$, $0 \leqslant x \leqslant \pi a$, $\frac{1}{2}\pi a$, $\frac{1}{12}\pi^2 a^2$.
$f(y) = (2/\pi)(4a^2-y^2)^{-\frac{1}{2}}$, $0 \leqslant y \leqslant 2a$;
$F(y) = (2/\pi)\sin^{-1}(y/2a)$.

22. 2.83, 2.30, 2, 1.70, 1.18 cm; 25.9, 39.7, 18.5, 10.4, 5.1, 0.4.

23. $f(x) = \frac{1}{2}$, $0 \leqslant x \leqslant 2$; $F(x) = \frac{1}{2}x$.
$\begin{cases} f(X) = \frac{1}{4}X,\ 0 \leqslant X \leqslant 2;\ F(X) = \frac{1}{8}X^2. \\ f(X) = 1-\frac{1}{4}X,\ 2 \leqslant X \leqslant 4;\ F(X) = X-\frac{1}{8}X^2-1. \end{cases}$

24. $\begin{cases} F(z) = \frac{1}{4}+\frac{1}{4}z, \text{ if } 0 \leqslant z < 1, \\ F(z) = 1, \text{ if } z = 1, \end{cases}$
$E(z) = \frac{5}{8}$, $\text{var}(Z) = 37/192$.

25. (*a*) $\int_{-\infty}^{\infty}\int_{-\infty}^{\infty} g(r,\theta)\,f(r,\theta)\,dr\,d\theta$.
(*b*) $E\{r-E(r)\}^2 = E(r^2)-\{E(r)\}^2$.
(*c*) $E\{[r-E(r)]\,[\theta-E(\theta)]\}$.
$f(r,\theta) = 2/(\pi a)$; a/π, $a^2(\pi^2-6)/6\pi^2$, $a^2(\pi-3)/3\pi^2$.

26. $E(X) = \lambda\alpha\theta+\mu\beta\theta$; $\text{var}(X) = \lambda^2\sigma_1^2+\mu^2\sigma_2^2+2\lambda\mu C$; $\lambda\alpha+\mu\beta = 1$,
$\lambda = \alpha\sigma_2^2/(\alpha^2\sigma_2^2+\beta^2\sigma_1^2)$, $\mu = \beta\sigma_1^2/(\alpha^2\sigma_2^2+\beta^2\sigma_1^2)$.

28. $y = -1.5x+11$.

29. (2, 1.61); $y = 0.497x+0.506$; (2, 1.5); 0.27 %.

30. See §152, page 136, *Statistics: A Second Edition of a Second Course.*
$G(\lambda)$ min $= S_{yy}(1-r^2)$ proves $(1-r^2) \geqslant 0$.
A simple case for which $S_{xy} = 0$, $S_{xx} = 0.08$, $S_{yy} = 20$ is as follows:

x	2.1	1.9	2.1	1.9	2.1	1.9	2.1	1.9
y	0	0	1	1	3	3	4	4

GLOSSARY

This summarises the statistical ideas and definitions taught in *Statistics: A Second Edition of a Second Course.*

α error. See 'Type I error'.

Analysis of variance. The calculation of the components of two-factor analysis of variance is summarised below:

r rows	c columns: 1	2	...	c	Row sum $\sum_c x_{rc}$	Square of row sum	Row sum of squares $\sum_c x_{rc}^2$
1	x_{11}	x_{12}	...	x_{1c}	R_1	R_1^2	s_1
2	x_{21}	x_{22}	...	x_{2c}	R_2	R_2^2	s_2
⋮	.	.	...	.	⋮	⋮	⋮
r	x_{r1}	x_{r2}	...	x_{rc}	R_r	R_r^2	s_r
Column sum $\sum_r x_{rc}$	C_1	C_2	...	C_c	T	ΣR^2	S
Square of column sum	C_1^2	C_2^2	...	C_c^2	ΣC^2	—	—

Cause	Sum of squares	Degrees of freedom	Mean square is an estimate of
Between the rows	$\frac{1}{c}\Sigma R^2 - \frac{1}{rc}T^2$	$(r-1)$	$\sigma^2 + c\sigma_r^2$
Between the columns	$\frac{1}{r}\Sigma C^2 - \frac{1}{rc}T^2$	$(c-1)$	$\sigma^2 + r\sigma_c^2$
Residual	$S - \frac{1}{c}\Sigma R^2 - \frac{1}{r}\Sigma C^2 + \frac{1}{rc}T^2$	$(rc-r-c+1)$	σ^2
Total	$S-(1/rc)\,T^2$	$(rc-1)$	—

Note that $c^{-1}\Sigma R^2$ becomes $\Sigma R^2 c^{-1}$ if c varies from row to row and similarly $r^{-1}\Sigma C^2$ becomes $\Sigma C^2 r^{-1}$ if r varies from column to column.

Bayes' theorem. Let $A_1, A_2, \ldots, A_n$ be a mutually exclusive and exhaustive set of outcomes of a random process, and B be a chance event such that $P(B) \neq 0$ then

$$P(A_r|B) = \frac{P(B|A_r)\,P(A_r)}{\sum_{r=1}^{n} P(B|A_r)\,P(A_r)}.$$

β error. See 'Type II error'.

Bernoulli's theorem. The theorem of which the Binomial distribution is a corollary. If the probability of an event occurring at a single trial is p, the probability of exactly r occurrences of the event in n independent trials is

$$\binom{n}{r} p^r(1-p)^{n-r}.$$

Binomial distribution. Suppose that the probability of an event occurring at a single trial is p and the probability of it not occurring is q then $p+q = 1$ and the probabilities

$$P(0), \quad P(1), \quad P(2), \quad \ldots, \quad P(r), \quad \ldots, \quad P(n)$$

of 0, 1, 2, ..., r, ..., n occurrences of the event in n independent trials are given by the terms of the *Binomial expansion*

$$(q+p)^n = q^n + \binom{n}{1}q^{n-1}p + \binom{n}{2}q^{n-2}p^2 + \ldots + \binom{n}{r}q^{n-r}p^r + \ldots + p^n.$$

The mean value of r, $\mu = np$ and the variance of r, $\sigma^2 = npq$. As n increases the Binomial distribution tends to the Normal. The minimum size of n for which the Normal distribution is a close approximation to the Binomial distribution depends on the value of p. The Normal approximation to the Binomial is quite good provided np and $n(1-p)$ are both greater than 5.

Central limit theorem. If random samples of size n and mean $\bar{x}$ are drawn from a population with mean μ and variance σ^2 the distribution of $(\bar{x}-\mu)/(\sigma/\sqrt{n})$ approaches *Normal* (0, 1) as n tends to infinity.

(Note that the approximation is quite good even when n is relatively small. For some parent populations $n \geqslant 15$ is necessary but for others $n \geqslant 5$ may be satisfactory.)

Chebyshev's theorem. Given a probability distribution with mean μ and variance σ^2 the probability of getting a value which differs from μ by more than $k\sigma$ is less than $1/k^2$. Alternatively, the probability of getting a value which differs from μ by less than $k\sigma$ is more than $1-1/k^2$.

Chi-squared (Pearson's).

$$\chi^2 = \Sigma\left[\frac{(O-E)^2}{E}\right],$$

where O is the observed frequency of a particular class and E is the corresponding expected frequency.

Coefficient of correlation.

$$r_{xy} = \frac{\text{Covariance}}{\text{Product of standard deviations}} = \frac{S_{xy}}{S_x S_y}.$$

r_{xy} differs significantly from zero (5 % level) if

$$t = r_{xy}\sqrt{\left(\frac{n-2}{1-r_{xy}^2}\right)} \quad \text{with} \quad \nu = n-2$$

is greater than the P (= 5 %) value of t in *Cambridge Elementary Statistical Tables* 3. For a given value of n,

$$r_{xy} = t/\sqrt{(t^2+n-2)} \quad \text{with} \quad \nu = n-2$$

gives the minimum value of $|r_{xy}|$ for correlation to be probable.

Coefficient of rank correlation (Spearman's).

$$\rho = 1-\frac{6\Sigma D^2}{n(n^2-1)}.$$

Coefficient of regression. The gradient of the regression line.
The coefficient of regression of y on x is S_{xy}/S_x^2.
The coefficient of regression of x on y is S_{xy}/S_y^2.

Combinations (or selections) $\binom{n}{r}$ **or** ^nC_r. The number of combinations of n unlike things taken r at a time is

$$\binom{n}{r} = \frac{n(n-1)(n-2)\ldots(n-r+1)}{1\cdot 2\cdot 3\ldots r} = \frac{n!}{r!\,(n-r)!}.$$

Confidence limits of the mean. The 95 % confidence limits of the mean are $m \pm (ts/\sqrt{n})$, where t is the P = 5 % value of the t-distribution for $\nu = n-1$ (sample of size n). Similarly the 99.8 % confidence limits are obtained from the P = 0.2 % value. The probability that the true mean lies outside the 95 % confidence limits is 5 % or $\frac{1}{20}$.

Covariance of a bivariate distribution. For n separate (x, y) pairs

$$S_{xy} = \frac{1}{n}\Sigma(x-\bar{x})(y-\bar{y})$$

$$= \frac{\Sigma xy}{n} - \left(\frac{\Sigma x}{n}\right)\left(\frac{\Sigma y}{n}\right).$$

For a grouped distribution

$$S_{xy} = \frac{\Sigma fxy}{\Sigma f} - \left(\frac{\Sigma f_x x}{\Sigma f}\right)\left(\frac{\Sigma f_y y}{\Sigma f}\right).$$

Degrees of freedom. In calculating the standard deviation of n observations the sum of the deviations from the mean is zero. Hence, when $(n-1)$ deviations have been written down, the nth deviation is determined and we say that for n observations there are $(n-1)$ degrees of freedom.

Exponential distribution. Suppose that incidents occur independently and at random intervals, the probability of an incident occurring in any interval δx being $\lambda\delta x$. The probability density function of the intervals between consecutive incidents, $p(x) = \lambda e^{-\lambda x}$, for which the mean interval between incidents is $1/\lambda$, is called the Exponential distribution.

***F*-test.** Suppose that two samples of size n_1 and n_2 have variances s_1^2 and s_2^2 which have been calculated by using $\nu_1 = n_1-1$ and $\nu_2 = n_2-1$ degrees of freedom and that $s_1^2 > s_2^2$. If the variance ratio $F = s_1^2/s_2^2$ is greater than the $P = 2\frac{1}{2}\,\%$ value of F for ν_1 and ν_2 given in *Cambridge Elementary Statistical Tables* 7(*b*) then the null hypothesis that the two samples are drawn from populations with the same variance must be rejected at the 5 % level. The *Cambridge Elementary Statistical Tables* also give $P = 5\,\%$, $P = 1\,\%$ and $P = 0.1\,\%$ values of F.

Interval estimate. A range of values which indicates the reliability of the point estimate of a parameter θ. If we can find two functions L and U of the sample values such that $P\{L < \theta < U\} = 0.95$ then the interval estimate (L, U) is a 0.95, or 95 %, confidence interval for θ.

Least-squares line of best fit. If $y = a + bx$ is the equation, the values of a and b are given by the *normal* equations

$$\Sigma y = na + b\Sigma x,$$
$$\Sigma xy = a\Sigma x + b\Sigma x^2,$$

where n is the number of (x, y) pairs.

An alternative form of the equation is

$$(y - \bar{y}) = \frac{S_{xy}}{S_x^2}(x - \bar{x}),$$

or

$$(y - \bar{y}) = \frac{r_{xy} S_y}{S_x}(x - \bar{x}).$$

Predictions of y based on the above equation can only be regarded as expectations. If α and β are the respective population values corresponding to a and b, the two-tail percentage points of the t-distribution, with $\nu = (n-2)$ degrees of freedom, can be used to obtain interval estimates of β, α and y. First calculate s_e, the standard error of estimate either by

$$s_e^2 = \frac{\sum_{r=1}^{n}(y - a - bx_r)^2}{n-2},$$

or by

$$s_e^2 = \frac{\Sigma y^2 - a\Sigma y - b\Sigma xy}{n-2}.$$

Then

(i) $t = \dfrac{|b-\beta|}{s_e}\sqrt{\left(\dfrac{n(\Sigma x^2) - (\Sigma x)^2}{n}\right)}$ gives the significance of $|b - \beta|$. Note that b is said to be significant if it differs significantly from zero.

(ii) $b \pm \dfrac{ts_e}{\sqrt{\left(\dfrac{n(\Sigma x^2) - (\Sigma x)^2}{n}\right)}}$ gives the confidence limits for β.

(iii) $t = \dfrac{|a-\alpha|}{s_e\sqrt{\left(\dfrac{1}{n} + \dfrac{n\bar{x}^2}{n(\Sigma x^2) - (\Sigma x)^2}\right)}}$ gives the significance of $|\alpha - a|$.

Note that if a does not differ significantly from zero the line passes through the origin.

(iv) $a \pm ts_e \sqrt{\left(\frac{1}{n} + \frac{n\bar{x}^2}{n(\Sigma x^2) - (\Sigma x)^2}\right)}$ gives confidence limits for α.

(v) $(a + bx_0) \pm ts_e \sqrt{\left(\frac{1}{n} + \frac{n(x_0 - \bar{x})^2}{n(\Sigma x^2) - (\Sigma x)^2}\right)}$ gives confidence limits for the *mean value of y* estimated from x_0.

(vi) $(a + bx_0) \pm ts_e \sqrt{\left(1 + \frac{1}{n} + \frac{n(x_0 - \bar{x})^2}{n(\Sigma x^2) - (\Sigma x)^2}\right)}$ gives confidence limits for an *individual value of y* estimated from x_0.

Level of significance. See 'Significance'.

Lower quartile. The lower quartile divides the area under the probability curve (not necessarily 'normal') in the ratio 1:3. The lower quartile is the 25th percentile.

Mean. The arithmetic mean, or more simply the mean, of the n values $x_1, x_2, \ldots, x_n$ is

$$\bar{x} = \frac{1}{n}(x_1 + x_2 + \ldots + x_n)$$

$$= \frac{1}{n}\Sigma x.$$

If the n values have respective frequencies $f_1, f_2, \ldots, f_n$

$$\bar{x} = \frac{f_1x_1 + f_2x_2 + \ldots + f_nx_n}{f_1 + f_2 + \ldots + f_n}$$

$$= \Sigma fx/\Sigma f.$$

For a *continuous probability curve* $y = f(x)$ $(a \leqslant x \leqslant b)$,

$$\int_a^b y\,dx = 1 \quad \text{and} \quad \mu = \int_a^b xy\,dx.$$

Mean deviation. The mean deviation of the n values $x_1, x_2, \ldots, x_n$ is

$$\frac{1}{n}\{|x_1 - \bar{x}| + |x_2 - \bar{x}| + \ldots + |x_n - \bar{x}|\} = \frac{1}{n}\Sigma|x - \bar{x}|.$$

If the n values have respective frequencies $f_1, f_2, \ldots, f_n$ the mean deviation

$$= \frac{f_1|x_1 - \bar{x}| + f_2|x_2 - \bar{x}| + \ldots + f_n|x_n - \bar{x}|}{f_1 + f_2 + \ldots + f_n}$$

$$= \Sigma f|x - \bar{x}|/\Sigma f.$$

For a *continuous probability curve* $y = f(x)$ $(a \leqslant x \leqslant b)$,

$$\text{mean deviation} = \int_a^b |x - \bar{x}|\,y\,dx.$$

Median. The median bisects the area under the probability curve (not necessarily 'normal'). The median is the 50th percentile.

Normal density function. The equation of the Normal density function in its most general form is

$$y = \frac{1}{\sigma\sqrt{(2\pi)}} e^{-\frac{1}{2}(x-\mu)^2/\sigma^2}.$$

Here, μ is the mean and σ the standard deviation and the distribution is known as *Normal* (μ, σ^2). Values of the Normal (0, 1) distribution are given in the *Cambridge Elementary Statistical Tables* 1.

Normal equations. See 'Least-squares line of best fit'.

Null hypothesis. The null hypothesis is the *assumption* which is made when applying a significance test.

Parameters. Constants appearing in the specification of probability distributions, e.g. p (Binomial), a (Poisson), μ, σ^2 (Normal), λ (Exponential).

Percentiles. The values which divide the area under the probability curve (not necessarily 'Normal') into a hundred equal parts. The 25th, 50th and 75th percentiles are known as the lower quartile, median and upper quartile respectively.

Point estimate. A single numerical value obtained from a random sample which locates a parameter θ such as the mean, standard deviation or correlation coefficient as a single point on the real number scale. A point estimate does not indicate the reliability or precision of the method of estimation. For this we need an interval estimate. The ideal point estimate T will be *unbiased* and of minimum variance. Also as the sample size increases the estimate T should converge towards θ. In this case T is called *consistent.*

Poisson distribution. The Poisson distribution is the form assumed by the Binomial distribution when p is small and n is large, the mean number of occurrences np being a finite constant a. In this case the probabilities $P(0)$, $P(1)$, $P(2)$, ..., $P(r)$ of 0, 1, 2, ..., r occurrences of the event are

$$e^{-a}, \quad ae^{-a}, \quad \frac{2!}{a^2} e^{-a}, \quad \ldots, \quad \frac{a^r}{r!} e^{-a}$$

respectively.

Power of a significance test. This is defined as $(1-\beta)$ where β is the probability of the Type II error. The power of a test increases as the size of the sample increases. The power tends to α as the true value θ tends to the assumed value θ_0.

Probability generating function. A function of t, usually denoted by $P(t)$, in which the probability, p_r, of r successes is the coefficient of t^r. The pgf of the Binomial distribution is $P(t) = (1-p+pt)^n$. The pgf of the Poisson distribution is $P(t) = e^{-a+at}$. The mean and variance of the distribution are given respectively by $P'(1)$ and $P''(1)+P'(1)-\{P'(1)\}^2$.

Quartiles. See 'Lower quartile' and 'Upper quartile'.

Sampling distribution. Suppose that all the possible samples of a given size are drawn from a parent population. The means of these samples themselves form a population whose distribution is called the sampling distribution of the mean. Such a sampling distribution exists not only for the mean but for any point estimate.

Selections. See 'Combinations'.

Sheppard's correction for grouping. When the mean and variance are calculated from a grouped frequency distribution, errors occur because each observation in a group takes the mid-value of the group. The final error in the mean is negligible because the positive and negative errors in the individual observations tend to cancel each other. In the calculation of the variance, owing to squaring, all the terms become positive. An allowance can be made for the error thus caused by grouping. It is to *reduce the variance by* $\frac{1}{12}c^2$ *where c is the length of the class interval.* This is known as Sheppard's correction. The formula for the standard deviation thus becomes

$$s = \sqrt{\left\{\frac{\Sigma fx^2}{\Sigma f} - \left(\frac{\Sigma fx}{\Sigma f}\right)^2 - \frac{c^2}{12}\right\}}.$$

It will be realised that 'working units' are often chosen so that $c = 1$. The correction only applies when the group intervals are equal.

Significance. The level of significance is the *probability*, stated as α %, which is calculated when making a significance test. For some tests, by using an appropriate formula, the level of significance may be obtained from t, χ^2 or F tables. In other tests, by assuming that the null hypothesis is true, we can make a direct calculation of the probability, α %, of all values of the variate which are as extreme as, or more extreme than, the observed value. If α is greater than the *arbitrary* value 5 it is usual to accept the null hypothesis as reasonable for the population being tested by the observation or sample. If α % is less than 5 %, it is usual to reject the null hypothesis. Significance tests can be applied in a great variety of ways. They can be made more stringent by taking $2\frac{1}{2}$, 1 or 0.1 as arbitrary values for α instead of 5 but they never completely prove or disprove the null hypothesis.

Significance of a single mean. To test the hypothesis that $\mu = \mu_0$ compare

$$t = \frac{|\mu_0 - m|}{s/\sqrt{n}}$$

with the percentage points of the t-distribution given in *Cambridge Elementary Statistical Tables* 3 ($\nu = n-1$).

Significance of the difference between means.

For large samples $$\frac{|m_1 - m_2|}{\sqrt{\left(\frac{s_1^2}{n_1} + \frac{s_2^2}{n_2}\right)}} > 1.96$$

For small samples

$$t = \frac{|m_1 - m_2|}{s\sqrt{\left(\frac{1}{n_1} + \frac{1}{n_2}\right)}}, \quad \text{where} \quad s^2 = \frac{(n_1-1)\,s_1^2 + (n_2-1)\,s_2^2}{(n_1+n_2-2)}.$$

Compare t with the percentage points given in *Cambridge Elementary Statistical Tables* 3 taking

$$\nu = n_1 + n_2 - 2.$$

Significance of variance ratio. See '*F*-test'.

Standard deviation. The standard deviation of the n values $x_1, x_2, \ldots, x_n$ is

$$s = \sqrt{\left\{\frac{\Sigma(x-\bar{x})^2}{n-1}\right\}}$$

$$= \sqrt{\left\{\frac{\Sigma x^2}{n-1} - \frac{n}{n-1}\left(\frac{\Sigma x}{n}\right)^2\right\}}.$$

For large samples ($n > 50$ say), $1/(n-1)$ is approximately equal to $1/n$. If the n values have respective frequencies $f_1, f_2, \ldots, f_n$

$$s = \sqrt{\left\{\frac{\Sigma f(x-\bar{x})^2}{\Sigma f}\right\}}$$

$$= \sqrt{\left\{\frac{\Sigma fx^2}{\Sigma f} - \left(\frac{\Sigma fx}{\Sigma f}\right)^2\right\}}.$$

For a continuous probability curve $y = f(x)$ $(a \leqslant x \leqslant b)$, for which $\int_a^b y\,\mathrm{d}x = 1$

$$\sigma = \sqrt{\left\{\int_a^b x^2 y\,\mathrm{d}x - \left(\int_a^b xy\,\mathrm{d}x\right)^2\right\}}.$$

Standardised deviate. The standardised deviate of a value x is $(x-\bar{x})/s$.

Type I and Type II errors. An erroneous conclusion to a significance test may be reached in two ways. We may

either (i) reject the null hypothesis, H_0, when it is actually true,

or (ii) accept the null hypothesis, H_0, when it is actually false.

These are respectively Type I and Type II errors. Their respective probabilities are always represented by α and β. Symbolically

$$\alpha = P\{\text{Type I error}\} = P\{\text{reject } H_0 | H_0 \text{ true}\},$$

$$\beta = P\{\text{Type II error}\} = P\{\text{accept } H_0 | H_0 \text{ false}\}.$$

The probability α is the level of significance of the test. It can be calculated from the value θ_0 of the parameter assumed in the null hypothesis and the data of the sample or experiment. The probability β depends not only upon θ_0 but also upon the true value θ of the parameter.

Upper quartile. The upper quartile divides the area under the probability curve (not necessarily 'normal') in the ratio 3:1. The upper quartile is the 75th percentile.

Variance ratio. See '*F*-test'.

Yates's correction for continuity. In the calculation of χ^2, if $\upsilon = 1$ the $(O-E)$ differences must be diminished numerically by $\frac{1}{2}$.

SOME SUGGESTIONS FOR FURTHER READING

Many excellent texts are available for students who wish to extend this study of statistical mathematics. It would be easy to continue almost indefinitely the following short list of authors, titles and publishers:

M. G. BULMER (1968), *Principles of Statistics*, Oliver & Boyd.

R. C. CAMPBELL (1967), *Statistics for Biologists*, C.U.P.

J. H. DURRAN (1970), *SMP Probability and Statistics*, C.U.P.

W. FELLER (1968), *An Introduction to Probability Theory and its Applications*, Volumes 1 and 2, Wiley & Sons.

J. E. FREUND (1971), *Mathematical Statistics*, Prentice-Hall.

P. G. HOEL (1971), *Introduction to Mathematical Statistics*, Wiley & Sons.

D. V. HUNTSBERGER (1961), *Elements of Statistical Inference*, Allyn & Bacon.

P. L. MEYER (1970), *Introductory Probability and Statistical Applications*, Addison-Wesley.

S. L. PARSONSON (1971), *Pure Mathematics*, Volume 2, C.U.P.

C. E. WEATHERBURN (1949), *A First Course in Mathematical Statistics*, C.U.P.

INDEX

The numbers refer to pages